"... And You Are Christ's"

THOMAS DUBAY, S.M.

". . . And You Are Christ's"

*The Charism of Virginity
and the Celibate Life*

IGNATIUS PRESS   SAN FRANCISCO

Cover by Marcia Ryan

With ecclesiastical approval
© 1987 Ignatius Press, San Francisco
All rights reserved
ISBN 0-89870-161-9
Library of Congress Catalogue number 87-80793
Printed in the United States of America

CONTENTS

PREFACE

The idea of virginity is not popular in the worldly world. What was formerly referred to as a woman's honor has in the erotomania of our day become almost a dishonor. It is often considered as a deprivation at best, an illness at worst. Nonetheless we shall in these pages retain the biblical word *virginity* with not the least apology for it. Because this term designates a primal, unspoiled, total readiness for one Beloved, there is no reason why we should allow the secular mind to co-opt a beautiful reality, reduce it to a mere physical condition, and then proceed to denigrate what it does not understand.

Evangelical virginity is always a consecrated freshness, a complete self-gift to the divine Beloved. It is also an ecclesial charism, for the individual virgin is a woman who lives in a calm but intense manner what the whole Church is, a virgin bride married to one Husband, Christ the Lord (2 Cor 11:2). She is a woman whose whole attention is focused on him, just as the Church has no other *raison d'être* than a profound love covenant

and communion with the Word and his Father
through their Holy Spirit.

A Word to Men

This biblical revelation posed a problem to me
when at the outset I had to decide on the precise
audience this book should address. On the one
hand virginity is not considered in our society as
a trait of men, even chaste men. For us a virgin
is a young woman who has preserved her chastity.
On the other hand there is no good reason why
one half of our population should be excluded
from what the New Testament and our theology
have to say about the positive grandeur of a complete chastity given to the Lord and to his people.

It is of course true that because of her feminine
nature and its typical traits the woman can image
and live the Church's wedded relationship to
Christ more realistically and more attractively
than can a man. But it is also true that the whole
Church, women and men alike, is a virgin wedded
to Christ, just as in the Old Testament the people
of God was a virgin bride wedded to Yahweh.

Just as on the natural plane women and men
differ widely in their outlook on reality, so too
do they vary in their attraction to the life of consecrated celibacy. Normal women are readily
drawn to the Pauline imagery of the Church as

the beautiful bride married to Christ. A woman's whole bent is toward persons and love. Drawn naturally to the male and his characteristics, a woman with the virginal charism and responding fully to its implications of a total, burning love for God, easily sees herself as given in a heavenly marriage to the eternal Word of God become man. She has no problem in seeing her life, not as an impersonal career—a job to be done—but as Saint Paul describes it, giving her undivided and chaste attention to one Beloved.

A man sees consecrated celibacy somewhat differently. His attraction centers on the towering and virile figure of Christ as one normal man is drawn, with not the least erotic overtones, to another extraordinary man—but immeasurably more so, for this extraordinary man is also the very Son of God. When the male responds fully to his celibate gift and thus begins to grow in a total, burning love for Christ, he sees himself not, obviously, as a bride, but as an intimate friend and brother. Such actually is another way Jesus addresses himself to his chosen intimates: "I shall not call you servants any more . . . I call you friends [beloved ones]" (Jn 15:15).

Yet men with the celibate charism need to be reminded that they, along with all men and women, are members of the virgin Church wedded to one husband. Before God each person is receptive, feminine. As a young man rejoices in his bride, so the Lord rejoices in his people (Is 62:5). And this bride-people, bedecked with her jewels, in turn rejoices with all her heart in her God (Is 61:10). Virile Paul not only speaks of the whole Corinthian church as a virgin wedded to the one husband, Christ Jesus, but also speaks of himself as being in labor as he begets them by proclaiming the good news (2 Cor 11:2; 1 Cor 4:15). The virgin Church is also Mother Church, and all of us are her members.

These pages therefore do envision celibate men who have dedicated their whole beings to God alone in and through the Church. Most of what we have to say applies equally to women and to men, and even in those sections that are best seen in the former proper applications will not be difficult for the latter.

While we are speaking specifically to men, it may be well to address a word to the allegation often made against the Church's requirement of celibacy for priests in her Latin rite. It is said that celibacy should be a free choice, a fully willed commitment. True indeed. It is also added that it ought not to be exacted or imposed as a price for the sacerdotal office. True again. It is further said that men should not be forced to forego marriage when they desire to serve God's people through the sacrament of orders. This argument appears persuasive to some people, but actually it has no substance. No one is forced to priesthood or to celibacy. In the first century we already read in the pastoral letters that the infant Church was aware that it could choose its leaders according to their marital status, that they be married no more than once (1 Tim 3:2; Titus 1:6). The Church in later centuries, aware of the same authority, has found it beneficial to choose most of its leadership from among those with the celibate charism, that is, from those who are not called to marriage at all. Knowing this decision and the divine authority behind it ("whatever you bind on earth . . .") men in the Latin rite are foolish to seek the priesthood if they do not have and gladly accept the celibacy. God does not fight the Church he himself established and authorized to act in his name. When he calls to the priesthood, in the Roman rite he ordinarily extends the call to those to whom he has already given the gift of celibacy. Since no one may claim the priestly office as a right, the Church is well justified in selecting her ordained leaders from those who freely and willingly choose celibate dedication. Nothing is imposed on them.

A Note for Women

Because this volume on its every page clearly envisions the consecrated woman, our comment here is brief. The female virgin enjoys a loftier place in the divine economy of salvation than is commonly supposed. Her feminine gifts and qualities eminently fit her for living concretely and imaging fully what the whole Church is, the virgin bride of Christ. While the ordained ministry of men is directly concerned with service, the virgin's role is directly pointed to a loving communion with the Lord himself. Her vocation lies at the core reality of the *ekklesia,* the biblical "one thing" to gaze on the beauty of the Lord (see Ps 27:4).

All the structures in the Church—offices, laws, institutions, chanceries, and curias—are aimed at fostering this core reality in all her members of both sexes. The consecrated woman's primary thrust is at the heart, the eternal immersion in the Trinity: "It will not be taken from her" (Lk 10:42). She has, therefore, a great deal to teach men about essential ecclesial reality, about how to be church, about how to love and nurture life and bring it to everlasting completion. It is disappointing in the extreme to see small, noisy groups of women clamor loudly for mere power, to see them losing something of their femininity as they strive to become like men, in the process neglecting or possibly in some cases despising their own womanly qualities, privileges, and destiny. Speaking of the lofty, Marian role women have in the Church, a role in which even males participate, for the whole *ekklesia* is feminine, Hans Urs von Balthasar remarks that the woman who would strive for the male role in the Church thus strives for something "less" and denies the "more" which she is. This can be overlooked only by a feminism that has lost the sense for the mystery of sexual difference, which has functionalized sexuality and attempts to increase the dignity of woman by bringing about her identification with man.[1]

Perhaps a word should be added to explain the immediate origin of this volume. Some readers will notice that several sections have previously appeared in the author's *A Call to Virginity,* a book that has gone out of print. A continuing need for it remains, however, and I have been pressed to attempt to meet this need in these pages. It has seemed better to go beyond mere republication by dealing with the subject in a more thorough way and by addressing several questions the previous work did not discuss. Hence, to a considerable extent *". . . And You Are Christ's"* is a new work, one which aims to meet the needs of young people who wish to give themselves entirely to God . . . and those of their elders who wish to grasp more adequately what their consecration means.

[1] *A Short Primer for Unsettled Laymen* (San Francisco: Ignatius Press, 1985), p. 94.

CHAPTER ONE

OUR MILIEU

This book deals with the most radical lifestyle one can imagine. It deals with a joy lofty and deep—so lofty and deep that most people have no concept of it, not even a clue. Virginity is radical and beautiful for the same reason that God is radical and beautiful. Though the world at large does not suspect it, gospel virginity is a love affair of the most enthralling type. It is a focusing on God that fulfills as nothing else fulfills.

Yet our subject is one of the least understood of all the truths revealed in and by the eternal Word of the Father. While consecrated virginity is not, of course, as profound a mystery as is the Eucharist, it is likely that most of the faithful could explain the latter more accurately than they could the former. Even priests and religious often have a surprisingly superficial grasp of why they are celibate, missing much of what the New Testament says of their vocation.

The world at large not only does not understand celibacy for the kingdom; frequently it is positively hostile to the idea. If a news reporter were to sound out representative public opinion in

London, Tokyo, or Chicago, he would probably receive three widely differing responses to the question, "What do you think of celibacy as practiced among Catholic priests, sisters, and brothers?" One person would dismiss the idea with words equivalent to "impossible, tragic, a pity". This respondent might mingle candor with bluntness: "Celibacy is unhealthy, unnatural . . . there must be something wrong with people who give up sex." While this first answer is secular and negative, the second might well be secular and positive: "I think it is noble that people could be so idealistic as to give up marriage to engage in scientific research, to aid the poor, or to teach in schools and run hospitals." The third view would speak of celibacy as a value because of the freedom it affords men and women to serve God in apostolic service. Though there would be differences in nuance, emphasis, and wording, it is likely that ninety-eight percent of the population would answer the question in one of these ways.

Two comments are in order. Celibacy is seen by almost everyone as a surrender, a giving up of "sex" and marriage. Even those who attribute to it a positive finality, think that it itself is nothing more than denying the sexual side of one's personality, the physical expression of that side. Second, in our imaginary survey no one thought of celibacy as a being in love with God, an eminently fulfilling, joy-bringing way of life, a new way of loving other men and women warmly and humanly. Yet this is precisely how the New Testament presents this vocation. We have here an excellent example of the biblical idea that merely human modes of thinking are far removed from the divine: "As the heavens are far above the earth, so are my ways higher than your ways and my thoughts higher than your thoughts" (Is 55:9). The divine thoughts about celibacy for the kingdom are no exception.

Few people suspect the beauty of gospel virginity. I do not refer simply to the virtue of chastity. Purity in any state of life is attractive, yes. But virginity is more than purity, much more than non-marriage—even non-marriage for a noble ideal. This is what few understand. This "much more" is the theme of our study.

Human thoughts and preferences are subject to the pendulum principle. They swing from one extreme to the other. In one decade isolationism is politically popular, in another it is internationalism. In one age consecrated virginity is so extolled by some writers that marriage is placed in eclipse. In our day marriage is so praised by some (although rejected by others) that consecrated chastity is either neglected or disdained. While this study commends virginal dedication, it should not be read as though it were belittling marriage. While both Jesus and Paul highly commend celibate chastity in both life and work, they cast no aspersions on marriage. Nor do we.

The resistance many parents offer to a religious vocation in their children is not all due to mere worldliness, selfishness, and a desire to see themselves in grandchildren. Much of it is due to sheer incomprehension. Part of this incomprehension is due to the fact that only rarely do we hear from the pulpit an enlightened explanation of perfect chastity. Homilies or sermons on "vocations" invariably stress apostolic needs. Almost never do they deal with the primary reason a healthy young man or woman gives up all things to follow the poor and celibate Christ. Another part of this general incomprehension is due to spiritual shallowness. Mothers and fathers with a deep prayer life instinctively see far more value in celibacy than do those who relate to God in a distant, cold manner. Sanctity brings insight into many mysteries—among them virginity consecrated to Christ.

Yet even holiness can be aided by lucid explanation. This volume attempts to render intelligible for all the faithful just what it is a young man or woman does in leaving everything, even the great gift of an earthly spouse. This surrender makes sense, of course, only in terms of getting someone still better in a new way, a way that includes the visible but stretches beyond it to the eternal. Only

God can give sense to so radical a life as is virginity, but the sense he gives "no eye has seen, no ear heard, nor has it entered the heart of man". To learn this meaning we must attend to the lips of the Lord, and this we shall do in these pages.

There is almost no literature on our subject aimed at intelligent young men and women. Most vocation brochures are far too sketchy and function-oriented. Religious life literature is often too complex, too shallow, or simply unavailable. While discussions of marriage abound, there is almost no adequate material written for the young who lack competence in professional theology and yet are capable of grasping far more than superficial presentations.

CHAPTER TWO

PRESUPPOSITIONS

O come to the Fountain all you who are thirsty.
(Isaiah 55:1)

We must begin with the beginning: you. As a human being, a spirit-in-the-flesh, you are a thirst (noun, not adjective). Every single choice you make all day long is proof that you seek, you desire, you want, you lack. Nothing is ever enough. You always want more of delightful experiences, and when the same experiences begin to wear thin and bore you, you seek new ones as well as heightened intensities of the old. You are engaged in an endless whirl. Always you seek, desire, want, lack.

Furthermore, you may have noticed that even after the most thrilling experience (a success, a vacation, a party, a date, a dance), when you are quiet and alone, you perceive deep down a small voice saying, "Is that all there is?" Nothing is enough: not praise, not success, not youth, not love. You are a thirst in the flesh, an incarnated thirst. You yearn for endless beauty and joy, endless love and delight, endless security and happiness—and an immortality in which to enjoy it all.

You cannot help being an incarnated thirst. Nor can I. We were born that way and we will die that way. We may differ in how we seek to slake our thirst. Some go up blind alleys. Others go to the Fountain. But all seek.

There are no differing vocations based on thirsting, seeking, desiring. All men and women want to be quenched, and any vocation must respond to the need for quenching. But there are differing vocations based on how efficiently and how rapidly the quenching is to be achieved. Jesus has said that those who give up family, property, and marriage for the sake of his enterprise achieve *many times over* even in this life (Lk 18:29–30). What they achieve must be what we now call "fulfillment": complete vitality, love, and joy. Christian celibacy is intimately connected with drinking at the divine Fountain, here and hereafter.

Vocation, Not Career

Aside from a few people immersed in the biblical word, our world has lost totally the concept of and feel for vocation. Yes, the word is used, but only because it has been first drained of a meaning that would elevate it above the notion of career. One of the basic mistakes some religious men and women have made in recent decades is to think of themselves as pursuing first of all a work to be done, a career. It seems not to have occurred to them that their life is precisely that, a life, an answer to a love call, a self-gift to a beloved. Not surprisingly they then go on to say that mission, not consecration, is the governing principle of their state in life. There is a partial truth here (namely, that mission is important), but it has lost full touch with the New Testament which insists that being is prior to doing.

While a career is a mode of making a living and contributing to the earthly welfare of the human community, a vocation is a call from the Divine Persons to a way of life. It is a beckoning, an invitation to give oneself totally to another person in accordance with the divine plan. Superficial writers and speakers could have thought of the idea of a temporary vocation only because they were not thinking of vocation at all. They were thinking of a career, an impersonal commitment to a job to be done. To be head over heels in love as a divine invitation seems to have escaped their vision of the evangelical counsels.

But it is not beyond the divine vision. From our mother's womb, indeed before we were conceived, each of us has been personally called to the universal and most basic destiny of an eternal, enthralling embrace with Father, Son, and Holy

Spirit, supreme Beauty: "With an eternal love I have loved you" (Jer 31:3). What this love entails for every individual man and woman and how we are to respond to it are presented in the pages of Sacred Scripture and the proclamation of the Church.

The most basic vocation is the call to love the Lord God with our whole heart, soul, mind, and strength (Dt 6:4–5; Lk 10:27). The destiny of the human person is an immersion in the bosom of the inner trinitarian life. This love enthrallment is of course the greatest of all the commandments, the very *raison d'être* of all men and women in every state of life.

However, this general vocation is to be made concrete according to divinely planned ways of life: the threefold radical counsels, the priesthood, marriage. Scripture does not present singleness as such as a vocation, for it does not include a self-gift to another. Rather it is a readiness for a self-gift. The God of revelation does call some men to the ministerial office in the Church. He calls some men and women to complete chastity, radical poverty, and a new obedience, all for the sake of the kingdom of heaven. And he calls others to marriage and family life.

A vocation therefore is to be sharply distinguished from a career, even though most people do pursue the latter as a source of livelihood and as a contribution to the welfare of the community.

For the sake of clarity we may point out several implications of this distinction.

First, a vocation is a result of the divine initiative. God invites one to a state in life. It is not simply a matter of looking about and "choosing what I would like to do in life". Certainly we would not say that God calls one to be a farmer rather than a baker or a lawyer, at least not as he calls one to priesthood, marriage, or religious life.

Second, the young man or woman approaches the question of state in life as a search for the divine will, not as a matter of selecting the most pleasing way of living. While one may pray about the selection of a career, he most decidedly must pray about responding to the divine call to a state in life.

Third, a state in life is a love matter, a *self*-gift to another, while a career is neither. A lawyer gives to a client advice, time, concern, expertise, but he does not give himself—nor does a doctor, baker, or engineer.

Fourth, a state in life (the result of a vocation) is a full-time matter, while a career is part time. A married man or woman is always a husband or wife; a priest and religious are always consecrated to the service of the Lord twenty-four hours a day. A teacher or nurse serves as such for a limited number of hours per day and days per week, and after a set space of time finally retires from the job. Husbands and wives, priests and religious remain married or consecrated day and night up to the moment of their deaths, even if and when they give up their work.

Fifth, a career is a means of securing a livelihood, for providing the material necessities of human existence on earth. While men and women pursuing a vocation usually enter some type of work as a means of monetary support, their state in life is something quite other than their technical skills.

Finally, a vocation is permanent; a career is temporary. A coal miner and a barber may leave their occupations whenever they wish, but in the divine plan they may not leave off being married. One may retire from the former but not from the latter. Why this is so we shall explain later.

Suppositions

We can understand conclusions only in terms of their suppositions or premises. One does not grasp either Communist or Christian conclusions until one has first grasped the principles of each system. We remain more or less blind to the meaning and beauty of Christian virginity unless we have assimilated the sublimity of Jesus' whole radical message.

The Son of God brought a revolution into the world, not just a polishing up of Aristotelian ethics. We are to be an altogether new creation, says Paul, not merely a refurbished old version (Gal 6:15). We are to renounce all that we possess, not just most of it (Lk 14:33). We are to be transformed from one glory to another, to the very image of divine beauty (2 Cor 3:18).

Virginity is a part of the altogether new creation. It is a sublime part. It is part of the revolution. We understand it only when we have first understood the revolution. That is why ninety-eight percent of the general population do not see the sense of virginity—they do not see the new creation with anything approaching adequacy. God's thoughts are still not our thoughts. You and I appreciate the surpassing beauty of gospel celibacy only when we appreciate the suppositions on which it rests.

What are those suppositions? One we have already mentioned: you and I are thirsts for God. We are thirsty with a thirst that nothing, absolutely nothing finite ever quenches. Jesus' teaching on celibacy supposes what the Psalmist long ago sang: "Only in God is my soul at rest" (Ps 61:1, 5). There is no resting, no fulfillment, no enthrallment, no completion anywhere short of an immersion in the triune life. Virginity takes this for granted.

The second supposition is that you and I are to be head over heels in love with God. All of us in every state of life are to love him as we can love no other: with wholeness of mind, heart, soul, strength (Lk 10:27). We are to be in such deep love that the eye of our mind is on him always (Ps 25:15), that we pray to him continually (Lk 18:1), that we sing to him in our hearts always and everywhere (Eph 5:19–20). This is the language of lovers. Admittedly. But the Christian virgin is to be a lover before anything else. This is why one does what he does. Only one who is in love gives up everything for the beloved.

The third supposition: a person's sexuality extends to every level of his being: physical, emotional, intellectual, volitional. Each of us feels, thinks, wills as a man or as a woman. We are told that each of our cells (even from a fingertip) has distinctively male or female traits depending on whether it belongs to a man or to a woman. Our discussion of virginity, therefore, must attend to its relation with human sexuality.

Our final supposition is that celibate dedication does not extinguish one's sexuality, but rather sublimates it. What is sublimation? It is the redirection of an energy from its immediate goal to a higher spiritual or social aim. If I am aggressive, I sublimate my aggressive tendencies from hostility toward others to a zealous concern for them. Sublimation of sexuality is not a suffocation; it is a rechanneling. Thus a virgin remains a woman with all her feminine gifts. She does not forget them, set them aside, or stamp them out. She rechannels them to higher, more beautiful purposes.

Once we understand these suppositions we are prepared to understand Christian virginity. Now this state in life is so rich a reality that we must unfold it step by step. There is no one brief, complete paragraph that can say it all. Because only God can teach it fully, it is suggested that you pray over what follows.

CHAPTER THREE

WHAT IS GOSPEL VIRGINITY?

Unless a person begins with a basic bias against chastity, he has no great difficulty sensing that a virginal life embraced as an ideal is somehow related to God. This perception may, however, be based on the misperception that the relation is due to the avoidance of something more or less tainted, that is, on the surrender of sexual activity in marriage. Not so. Evangelical chastity is the replacing of one noble love with another still more noble. It is the entry into a new sphere of existence, a privileged way of living the new creation brought into the world in Christ. His teaching by life and word is so rich a reality we shall unfold it with five leading concepts, all solidly rooted in the New Testament.

1. *Virginity: a Privileged Sphere of the Sacred*

To understand this first element in consecrated chastity we must take on the ancient Hebrew perception of God as the utterly Other, the wholly transcendent One, the supremely Holy One par excellence. The word for holy or sacred, *qadosh,* had a somewhat different meaning from what it has today. For us "holy" refers primarily to moral goodness: humility, patience, gentleness, temperance, honesty. For the ancient Hebrew it referred first of all to closeness to the All-holy One, to a being set apart from the ordinary creation and reserved in some special manner for the utterly Other, the Lord himself. Yahweh's people were "holy" not because they excelled in humility or temperance but because they had been called from the ordinary mass of mankind to a special relationship with the one God. "To me you shall be sacred; for I, the Lord, am sacred, I, who have set you apart from the other nations to be my own" (Lev 20:26). It is the divine selection, the setting apart, the consecration that makes them sacred. We find this same idea in the new dispensation. The faithful of Christ are sacred not because they surpass others in the moral virtues, but because they are a chosen race, a royal priesthood, a consecrated nation called out of darkness into the light of Jesus (1 Pet 2:9). We retain this usage today when we say a chalice is consecrated, not because it is of a higher quality of gold, but because it is set apart by a blessing for the exclusive use of the Eucharist.

God is so infinitely beyond anything created, so utterly other, so completely transcendent and sacred in and of himself that things or persons partake of his holiness simply by being called into a special closeness to him. Thus temporary continence was practiced in the Old Testament by priests before offering sacrifice and by men when fighting in a holy war, not because sexual relations in marriage were considered tainted, but because they belonged to the humdrum, everyday area of life in this world. To come close to Yahweh required a "retreat", a temporary separation from the merely created order. To worship the supremely Holy One in a suitable manner a man was to leave aside for a while his ordinary occupations. This tells him concretely that God is not merely the best; he is endlessly supreme, to be loved and adored for his own sake.

A virgin is a woman (or man) who is selected by the Lord himself from the generality of all other human beings to enter into the transcendental sphere of the utterly Sacred One in a new and exclusive manner, a manner that becomes a permanent state in life. When Saint Paul writes that the virgin is "holy in body and in spirit", he is not referring primarily to moral goodness, as though the married woman is not morally virtuous. He is making the point that she is selected from among women and is vocationally set apart for the sacred sphere of a complete preoccupation with God— while not, of course, neglecting her neighbor. In this sense she no longer belongs to this world, just as Jesus did not belong to it, but was entirely reserved to and for the Father (Jn 17:16).

Marriage and sexual relations within it belong to this world which is passing away (1 Cor 7:29–31), but the virgin anticipates the final age in which there is no earthly marriage (Mt 22:30), the final enthralling fulfillment of all human life. She is *qadosh* because even in this world she gives undivided attention to the Lord as her very way of life (1 Cor 7:35). She is a woman of the transcendent order of the supremely Holy One, for even now her whole thrust is to dwell in his presence, "to mind the things above, not those on earth" (Col 3:1–2).

Already we see that consecrated virginity is poles apart from the world's dismal, myopic view of it. The virgin who fully lives her vocation is vibrantly alive, much more alive than she could be with an earthly husband, for her Beloved is infinitely more alive than any mere man could be: her heart and her flesh sing for joy to the living God (Ps 84:2). We should believe the saints when they speak, write, and sing of the unspeakable delights of their love for God along with the painful purifications in prayer that make it possible. What they say is happening this moment upon our earth. Fire burns within these people.

2. Virginity: a Radical Readiness for and Pursuit of the Kingdom

The reader will understand as we explain the biblical concept of this state in life that, while we are dealing with no mere abstract idealization, we are decidedly supposing that the virgin is living what she professes. It is no argument against the biblical message to remark that there are celibate men and women who show little visible evidence that all we say here is true. Sadly, this is correct, but it misses the mark. One could as easily and as invalidly argue that battered wives (and husbands) together with widespread divorce prove that marriage lacks beauty and that sexual relations are a disaster. Commendation of a state in life supposes the normal case, and the normal case is that people are living what they have embraced in the way God intends it to be lived. Sin is abnormal.

The charism of celibacy changes a person from within. It readies a woman or a man in a radical manner for the ultimate purpose of all human life. We should note the key word *radical,* for baptism readies everyone for eternal life. The virginal consecration deepens this readiness, and it offers a way of life that sensitizes one to the operation of the Holy Spirit and for the more prompt pursuit of the kingdom that appeared in Jesus.

To appreciate this sensitizing readiness we need to note how fundamentally the values of the kingdom differ from those of the world. Otherwise we do not grasp the degrees of preparation for the former as against the latter. Indeed, we probably would not see that any preparation at all is needed for a complete acceptance of the radical gospel. We may illustrate this opposition with two values the world considers so obvious that they are widely assumed in technological societies as needing no proof. Advertising continually supposes that prestige—being considered beautiful, powerful, wealthy, influential, accomplished, and well known—is so important that it serves as one of the unspoken premises of the industry. For Jesus all this counts for nothing in the sight of God, since human opinion is a mere puff of smoke. The greatest in his kingdom are the humble, the downtrodden, the despised, and the nobodies: the first shall be last and the last first.

A second premise taken for granted in contemporary advertising is that money and all the pleasures it can buy, especially sensual pleasures, rank with prestige for top place in the hearts of most humans. In the kingdom, on the other hand, the love for money is condemned as the root of all evil (1 Tim 6:10), and wealth is said to make salvation almost impossible (Mt 19:23–26). While sexual activity in the divine plan is good in its proper place, it is so subject to abuse and tyranny that it must be regulated by a strict moral code. What is most highly praised is a perfect chastity and a factual poverty, both embraced for the king-dom.

No one with a moderately cultivated conscience is unaware of how deeply imbedded in our weak and wounded human nature are these two worldly premises and how vastly resistant we are to giving them up even mentally, let alone actually. Cling-ing to vanity and sensuality in all their intertwin-ing ramifications is the fundamental reason so few church-goers have a deep prayer life and make any notable progress in living as the saints have lived. Few people are ready for the radical pro-gram lived and taught by the Lord Jesus.

The main idea behind frugality and celibacy in Jesus' teaching is not freedom for apostolic work, important and valid as that is. Neither Jesus nor Paul speaks of the external apostolate when deal-ing with virginity for the kingdom. Rather they refer to a deepened state of being, of total avail-ability to the Lord's person and his enterprise, of a being sensitized to the new creation. It is signi-ficant that in Matthew's Gospel celibacy is linked with humility and poverty as fitting a person for the Christian enterprise. After Jesus invites some men and women to perfect continence (Mt 19:12), he goes on to say that only little children will enter his kingdom (Mt 19:13–15). Then come the two episodes of the invitation to factual poverty addressed to the rich young man and the almost insuperable obstacles the rich experience to entering heaven (Mt 19:16:26). What we have here is a threefold, radical emptying aimed at a greater readiness for accepting the message in thought and in fact. Just as humility and frugality sensitize us to the divine claims, so does celibacy. The three great emptyings of pride, material goods, and earthly marriage—emptyings which Jesus himself embraced—liken a person more fully to his mode of life and consequently produce a root preparation for what he is about.

Lucien Legrand has remarked that "the proper paraphrase of 'in view of the kingdom' would be: 'in order to *be* in harmony with the kingdom'. The voluntary 'eunuchs' are so because they have found virginity to be the condition that corresponds best to the nature of the kingdom."[1] In this state of being the disciple is of course more free to proclaim the message and to engage in the other works of mercy, but in the divine plan being always comes first, doing second (Mt 5:19; Acts 6:3–4).

It follows then that continence as a way of life is an anticipation of the final transformation where there will be no need for sexual activity, no procreation, no marriage. By being this anticipation, it becomes an apt sign of what everyone should pursue as our final destiny.

Saint Paul sees celibacy as a pattern even for the

[1] *The Biblical Doctrine of Virginity*, p. 44.

married, whom he invites to imitate it on a temporary basis. That is, he suggests that husband and wife through mutual consent may for the sake of deepening and extending their prayer give up this expression of their sexuality for a time (1 Cor 7:5, 29). In a similar vein the genuine widow is praised, not because her former marriage was an unfortunate state, but because she can now give herself up to continual prayer "day and night" (1 Tim 5:5)—devotion to prayer and more freedom for this is always the primary New Testament rationale for continence.

After the model of Jesus himself, the celibate man and woman are thus to be consumed by nothing but doing the Father's will (Jn 4:54). They have no other desire, no other ambition. They are utterly free for the kingdom, completely available to their sole love.

3. *Virginity, an Immediate, Ecclesial, Bridal Union*

We approach at this point an aspect of our subject that presents two problems to some people. Quite obviously, a bride must be a woman. Men therefore understandably feel that this element in celibate life is best left to women. This problem we have discussed in the Preface.

The second difficulty is the resistance some

women feel to what they consider a sentimental-
ization of their vocation. The terms wedding,
marriage, and bride when applied to vowed chastity bring to their minds images of a romanticizing
complete with gowns, lace, and rice. It is not their
concept of the evangelical counsels. If I may be
permitted to make a somewhat educated guess, I
would say that the preceding sentence strikes at
the core of their difficulty. If a study were to be
made of why some women resist the idea of virginity being a bridal relationship and if the study
could tap the unconscious, I would expect that
seeing their life as a career rather than a vocation
of being in love would emerge as the real source
of the difficulty. Surely religious who see their
life primarily, if not exclusively, as a job to be
done are likely enough to reject spousal love as
foreign to what they are about. On the other hand,
those who view their vows as chiefly aimed at
being in love with God are easily and naturally
inclined and attracted to the nuptial explanation.
As we shall shortly explain, this latter is the biblical
view of the people of God in general and the virgin
in particular.

Actually there is no more apt and normal image
of an intimate, total self-gift between two in love
than the spousal one. Biblical writers inspired by
the Spirit knew this, and they liberally used the
symbolism to describe the everlasting and unfail-
ing love of the Lord for his people. Isaiah speaks

of Yahweh delighting in his chosen ones as a bridegroom rejoices in his radiantly beautiful bride (Is 62:2–5). Hosea writes of this God wooing his wife in the wilderness that he may speak to her heart and win her back from her infidelity (Hos 2:16). The Corinthian church is for Saint Paul a virgin bride wedded to one husband, Christ (2 Cor 11:2; cf. Eph 5:25f.). Each member of the *ekklesia* is to cling so intimately to the Bridegroom as to become one spirit with him (1 Cor 6:17), and their love is to be absolutely total—to love with their whole mind, their whole heart, their whole soul, and with all their strength (Mt 22:37). It is a love so profoundly intimate that it brings about a profound inter-indwelling, each living within the other (1 Jn 4:16).

The individual consecrated virgin embraces a way of life in which she so exclusively focuses on her one Beloved that she declines a marital relationship with any other man. When Saint Paul explains who a virgin is, he makes this very point in three ways. First, he deals with virginity in a spousal context, immediately after considering earthly marriage. Second, he declares that the dedicated virgin is related to Christ as a married woman is related to her husband. Third, he indicates that she gives to him an undivided attention, which, as undivided, is a marital preoccupation (1 Cor 7:32–35). What the whole Church is to be, the individual virgin does by vocation and with no merely human spousal intermediary. She is a bride singlemindedly seeking her Beloved: "I will seek him whom my heart loves . . . I found him whom my heart loves. I held him fast, nor would I let him go" (Song 3:2, 4). Both the Hebrew and Catholic traditions have seen in the Song of Songs two valid interpretations: one a praise of ideal human marriage, the other the wedding between God and his people. Actually the first implies the second, given the spousal symbolism so common in both Testaments.

From the first centuries Catholic tradition has considered "the most illustrious portion of the Lord's flock" (as Saint Cyprian about 250 A.D. described consecrated virgins) as women wedded to no one but the Lord of the Church. The liturgy for virgin saints and for religious profession of women repeatedly summarizes this tradition and bestows on it the authority of universal worship. Saint Ambrose (fourth century) encapsulated the idea in his brief definition *"virgo est quae Deo nubit"* (a virgin is a woman who has married God).

We see an immediate consequence of this truth: a communion of love, deep prayer, and absorption in the Beloved must be the primary purpose of the virginal life. Neither Jesus nor Paul says a word about work to be done in reference to virginity, but they do speak about being in harmony with the kingdom, about focusing on the Lord in undistracted communion. The celibate woman or man, after the example of the Master, is to be a model of the Church at prayer. When we recall that Pope Paul VI defined the Church as "a society of prayer", we readily grasp why the virginal life is at the heart of the Church in her deepest reality.

4. *Virginity: the Fulfillment Vocation*

At this point, perhaps we had better anticipate an objection some people may have, lest it be a psychological obstacle to appreciating the New Testament message. We ought not, it is said, to compare the worth of vocations, and especially we should not assert that one is preferable to another. Since I have discussed this difficulty at some length in the book *Ecclesial Women,* we may be brief here.

It should be clear from the outset that when the New Testament and the Church both say that virginity for the kingdom is superior to marriage, they are comparing ways of life, not the value of persons before God. It is perfectly proper to assess the relative efficiency of diverse means as they more or less effectively contribute to achieving ends. Walking, cycling, motoring, and flying may rightly be compared as ways of getting from one city to another, and no reflection is made on the personal merits of the various travelers. States of life are obviously very different from one another, and it should not surprise anyone or hurt anyone to notice that they do vary in effectiveness in bringing the kingdom to fruition.

It goes without saying, of course, that it may well happen that a person using a lesser means may achieve more than one with a greater means— and vice versa. A saintly married man or woman is surely far greater in God's eyes than a mediocre monk or nun—and vice versa. But this does not change the plain fact that divine revelation does compare celibacy and marriage. Those who reject this truth are opposing both Jesus and Paul. They who give up property and marriage for the kingdom, says the Lord himself, get "much more in this present time" than if they do not, a clear comparison (Lk 18:28–30). A virgin, says Saint Paul, is in an admirable state, for she enjoys full freedom to focus her attention undividedly on God, and so the father who keeps his daughter unmarried does better than if he had seen to her marriage, another clear comparison (1 Cor 7:32–35, 38).

The Church, faithful to her Lord, likewise solemnly taught in the Council of Trent that virginity consecrated to God is superior to marriage. Vatican Council II several times used comparative terms to teach the surpassing excellence of consecrated chastity, and it expressly laid down that "seminarians are to be taught the superiority of virginity to marriage" (OT, 9). The reasons why this is true are so cogent that it would seem that only an a priori bias could prevent their being perceived in full force. I shall touch only one here and refer the interested reader to my book *Ecclesial Women* for the others.

Given that the primary reason for consecrated virginity is not work to be done but a deep prayer communion to be achieved, it is completely clear that celibacy lived as it should be lived provides more freedom both in time and in atmosphere than does marriage lived as it should be lived. Only a person who has known neither celibacy nor marriage in the concrete could seriously think otherwise. And we may take it for granted that any consistent Christian will agree with Scripture that a deep communion with the Trinity is the overriding necessity in anyone's life (Ps 27:4; Lk 10:38–42).

It has been objected with no little ineptitude that there are some married people who are holier and more prayerful than some celibate men and women. Of course—we all know such, perhaps by the dozen. But the remark proves nothing, for its reverse is also true. To compare the best of one group with the worst of another is no comparison at all. It is a fallacious and perhaps dishonest argument.

A final note. As canon law points out, a person cannot make a vow except for a greater good (Canon 1191, §1). They who oppose the teaching of the New Testament and the Church on vowed chastity are innocent of the theology of vows in general. Were one to follow their views, there would be no such thing as religious life.

We may now get on with our main concern: virginity is the fulfillment vocation par excellence. While marriage surely does lead to the human completion of husband and wife when and to the extent that they live according to the divine plan, evangelical poverty, chastity, and obedience even more effectively bring this completion about when and to the extent that they are lived authentically and generously. We may explain this "much more" in two ways.

Because the human person as spirit in the flesh breaks out into infinity, each of our desires for limited things implies a desire, usually unrealized at the moment, for the fullness of which the particular thing is only a tiny sharing. Reaching for a glass of ice water on a hot day is only a concrete expression of a deeper need for endless refreshment. Seeking to speak with a dear friend stems from a basic hunger to commune with divine love. Curiosity for news or the eagerness to look upon a splendid sunset emerges from a radical desire to gaze upon the Truth and Beauty who has revealed himself as attainable in the beatific vision.

The human person is therefore a thirst in the flesh, and virginity is the direct path vocation to the Fountain. Because it is on a straight line with no detours or distractions, it quenches more readily. Its lifestyle is tailored to attaining the "much more" in this life and eternal enthrallment in the next (Lk 18:29–30). The freedom of the virgin for the one thing makes it easier for her to "gaze on the beauty of the Lord" (Ps 27:4) and thus to rejoice in him always (Phil 4:4).

This vocation of fulfillment can be explained in another manner. Basing herself on divine revelation, the Church teaches that "the contemplation of divine things and an assiduous union with God in prayer is the first and principal duty of all religious" (Canon 663, see also Vatican Council II, CD, 33 and AGD, 18). In our theology the word *contemplation* means first of all infused contemplation, advanced prayer, not mere discursive meditation. Such also was the meaning Saint Teresa of Avila and Saint John of the Cross attached to the term. Men and women, therefore, take upon themselves the evangelical counsels of chastity, poverty, and obedience primarily and before all else in order more easily and freely to immerse themselves deeply into God through a prayer life that grows even into the transforming union. Of this we shall say more further on.

Suffice it to note here that it is this profound contemplation that feeds the human person in his deepest hungers, namely, hungers for truth, beauty, joy, celebration, love. People can be elegantly fed and clothed, can experience one pleasure after another to the senses, and always they end up empty, often miserable and jaded. Satisfying material needs contents mere animals, but it never contents human beings. The divorce and suicide rates among the wealthy are only the more striking examples, among others, that men do not live by bread alone. Infused contemplation is a divine inflow of beauty, truth, joy, and love. The Christian virgin embraces a way of life whose main purpose is to immerse her in the Divine Source of all truth, beauty, joy, and love. Her life must be the fulfillment vocation par excellence.

5. Virginity: an Excluding Fullness

Any Christian who examines what has been said thus far and what we will consider in our next section will readily grant that virginity in the divine plan is a fullness of vibrant living. When lived with generosity, it necessarily brings about the "much more" promised by Jesus himself to those who make the radical, total surrender. While this vocation is therefore preeminently positive, we must now notice a negative consequence, for any positive human choice necessarily includes negative results, other choices that cannot be made simultaneously. To choose to be in one place excludes being in another at the same time. To spend a sum of money in one way implies that that money cannot be spent in other ways.

The young woman (or man) with the celibate charism possesses a love-gift from God that so orients her person to him that she "cannot" give herself to another in a marital manner. This "cannot" is a special cannot. The young woman could reject the charism and marry, but she cannot reject it without doing some violence to her being. God has captured her as only he can capture. If she rejects his divine desire to possess her in an exclusive manner (God forces himself on no one), she hurts herself in that she turns her back on something that has been done to her. She refuses an interpersonal gift.

An example may help. If Susan is fully committed to James, her husband, she could, absolutely speaking, leave him for another man; but she could not do this without violence to her own being. In a like manner the virginal charism so focuses the young woman on God that she cannot give marital attention to another person. She has her fullness in the Lord.

A religious has well expressed this crucial "cannot". "It hit me suddenly", she wrote,

> that if my experience of God's life could make marriage almost an impossibility (because it would entail turning myself from one center to another—as though a woman would or could

marry two men and give them equal rights—it just can't be done), then it would not be quite accurate to say, as some do, that Christ chose celibacy [merely] in order to give a sign of dedication. . . . If one is being real, then it becomes natural to live celibately, since one's experience of God impels it and one would have to do some kind of violence in living otherwise.

This does not mean that the youth with this love-gift must already have a deep, advanced prayer life, but it does mean that God has already caught her attention in a special manner. He has given her, at least to an incipient degree, a focusing on himself that excludes a similar focusing on anyone else. Just as a faithful married woman may be attracted to another man, and yet focuses on no other than her husband, so also a virgin may be attracted to marriage and motherhood, but she knows that she can really give full attention only to the Lord Jesus.

John Henry Newman offers a striking example of our point. While he was still a young Anglican priest (and therefore free to marry), he was musing one day how wonderful it would be to have a devoted wife, one who would care about him and share in his aspirations and his thoughts. And yet immediately he added that he could not get married. His reason? He could not, he said, give the attention to the world that marriage requires. God had already captured his heart with the celibate charism, and he experienced the gift whereby he could not be concerned with the things of the world. His heart was too wide and deep, too centered on the divine.

When we turn to Saint Paul we find that this, too, is his explanation of why a Christian woman dedicates her virginity to the Lord. He does not say that she is free for function, a work, an apostolate. Unlike the married woman, who must be concerned with her husband and the world, the virgin is concerned with the "things of the Lord . . . , with giving him undivided attention" (1 Cor 7:34–35). Virginity is primarily a fullness in God.

When most people think of celibacy, they think in negative terms. For them this consecration is a non-experience of genital sexuality. It may be seen also as non-marriage for the kingdom. These negative concepts are true. But they omit what is most important, what is positive. To speak of virginity as a not-something is like speaking of Susan's marriage to James as a not-marrying of Robert or Philip and omitting to say that it is first of all a mutual self-gift with James.

The celibate person does give up an earthly marital relationship, but she is first described by the even greater relationship and fullness that she receives. It is a special intimacy with Christ that explains the "much more" fulfillment that she receives.

CHAPTER FOUR

UNDERSTANDING THE VOCATION

There are three levels on which one can grasp interpersonal realities such as trust, betrayal, friendship, loneliness, marriage, virginity, and theology itself. The surface level is merely verbal: words are learned and repeated by rote memory, but there is little or no comprehension. As a retention tool this can be useful for children who later proceed to levels two and three, but of itself rote learning is wholly inadequate. The second level is conceptual: ideas, definitions, and distinctions are understood mentally, and a great deal of raw information may be amassed, but the whole construct is sterile and lifeless. There is no inspiring and moving insight. Theologians who lack a vibrant prayer life may be competent technicians, but their understanding of revelation is thin and jejune at best, shoddy and erroneous at worst. One need only compare the love-penetrated and moving brilliance of Augustine, Athanasius, Thomas, Bonaventure, and Bellarmine with others who lack their sanctity. By an intriguing touch of Providence I was interrupted after the last sentence for breakfast here in York, England (a speaking engagement), and on my way back to my lodging the nun who served the meal called my attention to a nature poster with two lines that could not be more to our present point:

> If you do not understand my silence,
> You will not understand my words.

Exactly.

The third level of understanding is the experiential. While it supposes the conceptual grasp (there can be no human experience without intellect), it penetrates more deeply and with an emphatic connaturality. The mother who loves her sick child understands his whole situation more comprehensively and more deeply than a skilled doctor who does not love. Anyone who lives and loves a reality knows as the mere sterile non-lover cannot possibly know.

When we speak here of the signs of understanding the virginal charism, we are not thinking only of a grasp of the ideas presented thus far in these pages. In a similar manner, when we ask if a husband and wife understand marriage, we do not envision a mere capacity to read books and explain ideas. While the conceptual truths need to be grasped, of course, with their own rich insights, the experiential dimension and the connatural savoring are also necessary elements in the picture. We are therefore suggesting by what signs a celibate woman and man can know that they do see their vocation in a living way.

The first sign is a joyous non-reluctance regarding the sacrifices implied in the renunciation of all things for the sake of the kingdom. The sacrifices of marital love, home, family, and property are felt of course (one would be abnormal not to feel them to some extent), but the surrender is joyfully made. A person who spends a large sum of money for a treasured object feels the loss of the money because there are a dozen other items he cannot now buy with the same sum. But he is so happy with his treasure that he is by no means sorry to have made the sacrifice it necessitated. Jesus himself has put the matter perfectly: "In his joy he goes and sells all that he has and buys that field" (Mt 13:44). In a similar manner, a happily married spouse misses the warm family he or she has left behind, together with the many freedoms attendant on single life, but there is joy in the surrender. The virgin has given up earthly marriage and motherhood, yes, but she has entered upon a still greater marriage and motherhood. The sacrifice of the first may hurt, but there is no reluctance, for the attainment and experience of the second bring their own lofty love and fulfillment. The celibate man or woman understands his vocation when this joyous non-reluctance characterizes his day-by-day living.

The second sign is the experience of the "cannot" of which we have spoken, the inability to give to the world the attention that marriage requires. Even if the celibate is at a considerable distance from heroic holiness, he should feel at least something of being captured totally by the Lord for the concerns of the Lord. In a similar manner if a man is completely in love with his wife, he may find another woman attractive, but he could not possibly turn his serious attention away from the former because of the latter. So likewise the virgin who is thoroughly a consecrated virgin may find a man charming, but she could not possibly entertain serious marital thoughts about him. Nor can she be concerned about fine clothes, jewelry, and hairdos—the things Jesus himself said no Christian is to be worried about (Mt 6:31–34; see 1 Pt 3:3–5). This cannot is implied in Saint Paul's remark about giving undivided attention to the Lord: a person absorbed in another with the totality of consecration cannot suffer a division of mind or heart.

An ability to see through the superficiality of superficial things is a third indicator of grasping the celibate life. A person whose whole being is focused on the Alpha and Omega naturally enough sees all else in perspective. The saint, married or virginal, sees peripheral matters as peripheral. Saint Francis threw all his wealth and luxuries aside in a dramatic scene of renunciation because he was a man in love. He saw elegant dining and drinking, splendid clothing, and endless amusements as leading nowhere, and so he consigned them to the outer darkness. Francis understood celibacy because he understood what it is to be in love.

The fourth sign is the consequent freedom from being caught in compensation compromises. Perhaps the most subtle danger for men and women who have given up the values of married love, private property, and the self-disposition of their persons is the gradual, almost imperceptible drift into compensation seeking. Wounded human nature does not easily surrender tangible things in exchange for the invisible God. No sooner have we given up one thing than we tend toward a substitute to fill the gap. Physicists say that nature abhors a vacuum; so does human nature. This is why the absence of compensation compromises is a sign of understanding a vocation. Virginity is the love vocation par excellence, and one who is full of love has no vacuum to be filled. There is no need of substitutes, no desire for frivolities, no inclination to superfluities.

What may the compromises be? Absorption in a hobby. Excessive recreation. Useless reading. Idle chatter. Ardent pursuit of culture or social contacts. Workaholism. Overeating. We should notice the qualifications: absorption, excessive, useless, idle, ardent. We are not finding fault with a hobby, recreation, reading, conversation, culture, or work. While these are all respectable activities, making ends of them is not. A husband who spends far more time on the golf course than with his wife or a wife who prefers endless socializing to her husband obviously does not understand the covenant of marriage. So also the celibate man or woman who turns recreation, eating, chatting, culture, or work into an end shows little existential grasp of his vocation. The same, of course, is equally true of harmful compensation compromises: drink, sexual entanglements, authoritarianism. Men and women in love with God are free from all these illusory pursuits. They understand what they are about in life.

The most important of the signs, however, is a love for prayer, a devotion to contemplative communion. People in love are drawn to communion with the beloved. The model of all celibate dedication "would habitually go off where he could be alone and pray" (Lk 5:16). The model of all feminine virginity was noted for pondering the divine mysteries in her heart (Lk 2:19, 51), for being engaged in continual prayer (Acts 1:14). We instinctively know that a husband and wife who enjoy each other's company understand their marriage, and we just as well grasp that the priest (or nun) who is drawn to long (even if difficult and dry) prayer well understands his way of life. All chastity—marital and virginal—is directed to love.

We should notice, of course, that this communion in love will be found with the other four signs—or they will all be absent together.

CHAPTER FIVE

PERMANENT FIDELITY

Living as we do in an age of accelerated change, the age of future shock, we find a growing resistance to the concept of stability and permanence not only in the sphere of matter but now even in that of the spirit. Process theologians of the extremist variety carry their idea even into the Godhead, where it cannot possibly have a place. It cannot be a surprise, therefore, given the temper of the times, that sooner or later some few at least would be denying permanency not only in marriage but also in dedicated celibacy.

Before we examine what revelation has to say about the question of fidelity and permanency, it may be useful to touch upon the reasons behind the recent theory of temporary vocation. Why has it been left to our day to conjure up an idea so foreign to the gospel message of a radical following of Jesus, who is the same yesterday, today, and forever? We have already touched upon one reason, the temper of our times, admittedly a shaky motive at best. History makes it clear that in matters theological passing fads are no argument at all.

Nevertheless, attempts have been made to explain why the vocation to celibacy may be temporary. It has been said, for example, that people ought not to dispose of their whole lives with one act of the will, that they should leave their options open as they respond to changing circumstances. Others have noted that young people today find greater difficulty in making permanent commitments to anything, and the implication seems to be that allowance for this growing difficulty should be made in celibate dedication as well as in marriage. Neither of these attempts bears scrutiny. On the one hand we shall indicate below that leaving vocational options open can lead to a most unhealthy drifting, and on the other hand there is no evidence at all that permanent human relationships are significantly and essentially more troublesome now than they ever were. Attitudes toward commitment have changed in many cases, but not basic human problems.

On a less tangible and realized level lie two other motives for the theory of temporary vocation. One of these is the understandable desire to explain in favorable terms the enormous number of departures from religious life and priesthood in recent decades. One does not like to say that tens of thousands of men and women have been unfaithful to publicly made vows. It is far more pleasant to explain that God called them to celibate life for a while and then pointed out new ways to them. This comfortable explanation does not have any foundation in revelation, but it does attract on a superficial level.

The other less-realized motivation underlying the idea of temporary virginity is the viewing of religious life as a career rather than as a vocation. The problem with this idea is the premise, not the logic of the conclusion. Indeed, if celibacy were only a career, it would be by nature a temporary matter, for no one need be a dentist or a plumber all through life. However, as we have shown earlier, consecrated chastity is a vocation and by no means merely a means of making a livelihood or of serving others.

We turn now, therefore, and ask why this vocation is permanent, why one does not embrace this life for a while and then perhaps switch to something else. The first reason is that virginity is a total self-gift or it is not Christian virginity. The very concept of temporary virginity is a self-contradiction. As a contemporary theologian put it, virginity is

> a readiness for total commitment to another person. The virgin in this sense is one who has not dissipated himself or herself with temporary liaisons but has maintained a personal integrity to be given totally to another person. Virginity is thus not simply a matter of bodily integrity; rather, bodily integrity is a sign of the personal integrity that the virgin presents to the beloved

to whom he or she totally commits himself/
herself. Virginity is thus a gift of the whole
self.[1]

This totality of virginity requires therefore that
the self-gift be permanent, for a self-gift on a temporary basis is merely partial.

A second reason follows on the first and is
bound up with it: a total self-gift must be a love-
gift. And love here means love, that is, not a mere
strong attraction. Anyone who has been in love
knows quite well that the intent of genuine love
is an eternal intent. If a normal man and woman
agree to "marry for a while" or "as long as things
work out", of one thing we can be confident: they
are not in love, at least not in the full human and
divine sense of the term. C. S. Lewis put it well
when he remarked, "Love makes vows unasked".
Scripture reflects this truth in its insistence on unending fidelity to the beloved. "Set me as a seal
on your heart, as a seal on your arm; for stern as
death is love, relentless as the nether world is devotion; its flames are a blazing fire. Deep water
cannot quench love ..." (Song 8:6–7). In his famous chapter on love Saint Paul writes that love
"endures *whatever* comes", for it "does not come
to an end" (1 Cor 13:7–8).

Not surprisingly the New Testament sees per-

---

[1]Patrick Bearsley, S.M., "Mary, the Perfect Disciple",
Theological Studies (September 1980), 499.

manence as essential to the radical following of Jesus. Beginning with the Lord himself, who remained committed to his celibacy to death and for eternity, so the disciples, who left all things to follow him, left them for life and for eternity. In that total surrender, of course, was the giving up of marriage and a natural family, and this they did with a radical and temporal finality. Indeed when one follows the Lord he does not even look back, let alone go back. The person who begins but looks back is not fit for the kingdom (Lk 9:62). The evangelical counsels are a radical deepening of the baptismal consecration and thus a more profound entrance into the paschal mystery of Jesus' Passion, death, and Resurrection. Just as the eternal Son gave himself up to the sole possession of the Father and that for all eternity, so those who live this radical self-gift with and for him do it with no temporal limit whatever.

A fourth reason lies in the fact that consecrated virginity, itself a nuptial union with Christ, is a sign of the unbreakable union between Christ and his Church. To be this sign it must itself be permanent by its nature. Vatican Council II reminds religious of this fact when it says that "their consecration will be all the more perfect in the degree that, by bonds firm and unshakable, it better reproduces the image of Christ bound to his Church by a union beyond dissolution" (LG, 44). We should note, too, that the complete intimacy of a marriage requires mutual commitment without temporal break. Vocations are like that; careers are not.

The permanence of vocations answers the deep human need for stability, focusing, and direction. Supposing that one is adequately instructed and prepared, it is psychologically as well as spiritually healthy to dispose of one's life with a single, decisive act of will, an act that draws together the present and future into one unity. This solemn act of will (the marriage ceremony, the act of ordination to the priesthood, the profession of vows) makes a whole out of one's life and focuses one's attention and energies on a worthwhile purpose. People who refuse permanent commitment (unless for some unselfish reason) cripple themselves as persons. It is likely that they will lack drive, determination, and enthusiasm. Drifting is not healthy.

Finally, we know that consecrated virginity is a permanent way of life because the Church's teaching and practice through twenty centuries cannot be wrong in so important a matter. Under the guidance of the Holy Spirit she has always known that both the individual and the community need vocational fidelity if they are to prosper. She likewise knows the mind of her Lord, for the Spirit has been given to lead her to all the truth (Jn 16:13).

CHAPTER SIX

VIRGINITY AND FRUGALITY

Authentic things make coherent wholes. Their various parts and elements fit in with one another, indeed call for one another. The longer one studies divine revelation, the more he sees the analogy of faith in action: each mystery enters into all the other mysteries. The Incarnation, for example, calls for a virginal motherhood; the virginal motherhood of God calls for an immaculate conception, and all of these point to the fittingness of incorruption for this spotless virginal body, Mary's assumption into glory after death.

So too does consecrated virginity find its meaning in the Incarnation of the eternal Son. So likewise does it enter into other aspects of evangelical reality. Several of these relationships we have already noted. One more remains to be pointed out: virginity calls for gospel frugality. It is no accident that the three vows of religious life are chastity, poverty, and obedience. When groups of celibate men or women desire to live their consecration in community, there arises a need for a new authority/obedience relationship among them, a relationship that is evangelical because the community itself is based on the evangelical principles of virginity and poverty. It is the bond between the last two that we examine here.

There is an intrinsic connection between these two ideals, so intrinsic that the one requires the other in the nature of things. This requirement we can see in several ways. One is that the New Testament itself presents them as intimately related. Matthew deals with the three great renunciations—of marriage, pride, and possessions—one after another, in relation to the attainment of the kingdom; pride must be surrendered by absolutely everyone, marriage and property by a chosen few (Mt 19:10f.). The first is a command; the second and third are counsels. Luke, in reporting Jesus' saying about giving up marriage and possessions, juxtaposes continence and poverty as leading to the "much more" in this present age and eternal life in the next (Lk 18:29–30). Celibate Paul rejoices that, having nothing, he possesses all things (2 Cor 6:10), and he explains that the virgin of Christ is not concerned about the things of the world, for she is a poor woman wedded to a poor Lord. She has no care for wealth, jewelry, and feminine finery, for her whole attention is on him (1 Cor 7:32–35). And more important than anything else, the celibate Lord himself freely chose to unite a drastic poverty to his consecration. God does nothing by accident; there is an intimate connection between his celibacy and his poverty. And so it is too with his most radical disciples.

History, past and present, illustrates this connection, for religious orders flourish when they are poor; they decay when they are wealthy. One needs only to read of the past and observe the present to find evidence in abundance that chastity requires poverty if it is to grow, blossom, persevere, and endure.

The Fathers of Vatican II saw this truth, for every time they spoke of celibate groups in the Church (bishops, priests, religious) they spoke also of factual frugality. Bishops are to live so frugal a life that it is to be an example of simplicity to the faithful (CD, 15), and their dwellings are to be so unpretentious, so modest that the poor find no cause for apprehension when they enter them. Diocesan priests are invited to live a voluntary poverty, and they are told, not simply invited, to give away to the Church and charity the money that remains after their needs are cared for. In other words priests are to have no superfluities (PO, 17). Religious are told in bald, plain language to be poor in fact and in spirit (PC, 13).

The faithful, indeed those outside the Church as well, also entertain the conviction that celibates who are celibate for a religious ideal should go all the way and give up wealth as well. Ordinary men and women may not have studied a theology of the counsels, but their sense of reality prompts them to know that there is an intimate tie-up between the two ideals. They are quick to criticize the priest with his large car and expensive winter vacations and the nun who indulges in an extensive wardrobe. They are not edified by celibate men and women who eat, drink, and recreate on the level of the upper middle class. Behavior they do not condemn in their married friends (and in themselves often enough) they gossip about when they find it in clergy and religious. And if the latter do not think the gossiping goes on, they do not know their people. This kind of talk may be wrong, but it does illustrate how ordinary people easily see an inconsistency that their leaders choose not to see.

This inconsistency is our final point. There is something deeply abnormal in a man or woman who gives up the great interpersonal good of marriage and then pursues mere nonpersonal things. If one gives up a wedded human love, it can only be for a greater love, the love without which no person in any state of life is fulfilled, the love of God. To make clothes, property, or amusements one's end in life, to substitute finite gods for the infinite, sole God bespeaks an illness in a person made for love, an illness unto death. There is an intercausality between celibate love and evangelical poverty, for each contributes to the existence and well-being of the other. On the one hand the virgin who is achieving her purpose of being full of love simply does not care for things pursued as ends. She uses them sparingly and with a great inner freedom because her heart is elsewhere. On the other hand, as she lives frugality and detachment, she is all the more free to fall in love. She is an entirely healthy person.

For celibate women and men who proclaim the gospel there is still another inconsistency. Jesus' message is entirely an otherworldly message. While we should look after the material needs of our brothers and sisters and while we ought to further the betterment of our earthly city, we remain pilgrims pure and simple (Heb 11:13–16; 1 Pet 2:11). We are an ascetic people who tread the hard road and enter the narrow gate that leads to life (Mt 7:13–14). Celibate men and women who live comfortable, self-indulging lives make themselves look foolish if and when they proclaim the self-denial and mortification of the gospel. Their rhetoric about justice and peace in the world, about concern for third- and fourth-world poverty impresses no one when they themselves are dressed elegantly in the latest fashions, and when everyone knows they live on a level far beyond the necessities. What happens, of course, in many cases is that worldly celibates, being conscious that their life contradicts the gospel, simply refrain from talking about self-sacrifice and unworldliness. But then the inconsistency and inauthenticity are apparent in their silence. Everyone knows they should proclaim the integral message first by deed, then by word. Indeed virginity calls for frugality. "What we have to do is give up everything that does not lead to God" (Titus 2:12).

CHAPTER SEVEN

VIRGINAL HUMAN LOVE

> You have a permanent place in my heart, and
> God knows how much I miss you all, loving you
> as Christ Jesus loves you.
>
> (Philippians 1:7–8)

We humans tend to fear the unknown. We also
tend to have weird notions about the unfamiliar.
Possibly the most fearful and weird thoughts
about virginity float around the question of human
love. Does a celibate love warmly and humanly?
Does a priest or nun really love God only and
more or less "be nice to" men and women, without actually caring much for them? Is it possible
to love without sexual involvement in a genital
sense? Does the celibate mode of life stifle the
expression of warm affection or does it further it?
Are close friendships with members of the oppo-
site sex compatible with virginal consecration? If
they are, what kind of friendships are they? Does
an attraction to married love and parenthood indicate that a young woman or man has no vocation
to consecrated chastity?

No human love is mere attraction, not even
a strong attraction. The divine concept of love

73

implies a self-giving to another and it requires a developed maturity, a detachment from all one's petty clingings. Peter has it that we cannot (not simply, do not) love one another as we ought until we have accepted God's revelation and have been purified in soul (1 Pet 1:22–23). This is why until we love God totally, until we live what Saint John of the Cross explains in the *Ascent of Mount Carmel,* we cannot love our neighbor as we ought. If I "love" another because he/she "loves" me, I am loving myself, not the other. Virginal love therefore is not genuine unless it has four traits.

Characteristics of Celibate Human Love

Virginal caring is first of all a living response given by the Holy Spirit, who pours out genuine love into our hearts (Rom 5:5). It is a holding others dear as the celibate Lord holds them dear, for we are to give ourselves to them as he has given himself for us (Jn 13:34–35). Celibate Paul tells the Philippians in an affectionate passage that he loves them as Christ Jesus loves them (Phil 1:7–8). God therefore is the genuine motive of genuine love. The Apostle addresses the Romans as "God's beloved in Rome" (Rom 1:7). This may sound merely pietistic, but it reflects the actual truth. There is nothing lovable in the Romans or in anyone else except what radiates from the infinite lovableness of God and flows from him at every moment. There is no real way of caring for anyone except in and for Supreme Goodness, for no one exists except in and for him.

Second, celibate love is universal. While it obviously is bestowed on individuals as individuals (one does not love a formless humanity), it is not so focused on one that it excludes others from its ambit. Married men and women are to go out to everyone in sincere concern, but there is only one person who is the object of their marital love, that is, the spouse. Wedded love is by its nature limited to one; it is exclusive and possessive; it is to be given to no other. Virginal love on the other hand is by nature non-exclusive, unlimited. It relives the very self-giving of Jesus which combines individuality with warmth, intensity, and universality. The virginal heart is a large heart, too large to be satisfied in focusing on one man or woman.

Third, this affection is feminine in a woman and masculine in a man. Their caring is not some sort of neuter reality, and yet at the same time it obviously has no erotic or genital suggestions or tendencies.

Finally, celibate love is warmly shown; it is affectionate. While any genuine warmth implies restraint, limitations on expression do not translate into coldness. Men and women of deep prayer know instinctively where to draw the line that separates properly shown marks of affection from the improper. This warmth and universality are beautifully seen both in Jesus and in Paul. The Lord hugs little children before he blesses them (Mk 10:16), and he looks with love on a young man who is going to refuse a personal invitation to radical poverty (Mk 10:21). He pictures the father of the prodigal son as receiving the young sinner back with an embrace and a kiss (Lk 15:20). He feels deep compassion for the crowds and for the widow who lost her son in death (Mk 6:34; Lk 7:13). He weeps over Jerusalem (Lk 19:41), and at the tomb of his friend Lazarus (Jn 11:33–36).

Celibate Paul relives the warm affection of his Master. He can weep out of love in writing a letter (2 Cor 2:4). Though he is virile and fearless in facing enemies, torture, and death, he does not hesitate to use all sorts of endearing terms: God's beloved, my brothers, my children, my joy, my crown, dearly beloved. He teaches that Christians should be affectionate and greet one another with a *holy kiss* (1 Cor 16:20; 1 Thess 5:26). His farewell to the elders of Ephesus was characterized by tears, embraces, kisses (Acts 20:36–38).

It need hardly be said that all four traits— divinely motivated, universal, feminine or masculine, affectionate—are to be found together if celibate love is to be entirely Christian. Two or three are not sufficient, for authenticity demands wholeness. Real things are total things.

Sublimation of Sexuality

Look to the Lord and you will be radiant with joy.
(Psalm 34:5)

Virginity does not suppress sexuality but rather raises it to a new level of expression. Psychologists call this sublimation, a redirection of an energy from its immediate goal to another loftier social or spiritual purpose. If I sublimate my aggressive tendencies, I rechannel them from hostile attitudes to loftier purposes of solid achievement in work or prayer.

The Christian virgin appreciates her sexuality and she does not try to forget, suppress, or destroy it. She rechannels her sexual drives from a genital expression to a wider freedom for universal affection and profound prayer-love.

Some people need a genital expression of sexuality. They are called to marriage. Others, gifted with the celibate charism, do not need this expression. These latter are fulfilled in their universal warmth, in their special friendships, in their sacrificial love, but mostly in a communion with the Lord that is to make them *radiant with joy*. Jesus himself promised that those who give up property and marriage for the kingdom get *many times more* even in this life. History, past and present, gives eloquent testimony to his word. Celibates who live their vocation to the hilt, and thus attain a profound prayer-transformation, are marvelously fulfilled persons. Their sexual inclinations and energies have been raised to a new level of completion both in their universal love of others and most of all in a depth of prayer which eye has not seen nor ear heard. The saints are standing witnesses to this reality.

Special Friendships

Given that virginal love is universal in the sense we have explained and given that most who live this charism share it in community, it would seem on the surface of things that there could be no room for close friendships. But actually the question of special friendship poses no more problems here than it does for married couples. We may ask of them also, given the exclusiveness of wedded love and given that it is lived in a special family community, whether husband and wife may have other close relationships outside. The question is sharpened by the Pauline admonition that any follower of Christ is to "treat everyone with equal kindness" (Rom 12:16). If we are as attentive to and cordial and generous toward everyone in our immediate circle as we are toward our friend, one may ask what is special in the latter relationship. The person who finds this last question a real problem has lost sight of the deepest root of friendship, but to that we shall return a bit further on.

We know that celibate dedication is compatible with special friendships because the Model of all dedication had especially close associates. We read in the Gospel that Jesus loved Martha, Mary, and Lazarus in a unique manner (Jn 11:5). He loved everyone uniquely, of course, but there was something distinctive in his closeness to these two sisters and their brother. We likewise notice in the Fourth Gospel that the Lord had a marked fondness for the evangelist John. We find the same message among the saints: Catherine of Siena and Raymond of Capua, Teresa of Avila and Jerome Gracián (and other priests, laymen and women, and nuns), Jordan of Saxony and Diana, Francis de Sales and Jane Frances de Chantal. These are the names most commonly cited in writings on celibate relationships, but actually the more one reads the lives of the saints, the more he finds that close friendships are the rule and by no means the exception. When the official Church examines the lives of these men and women, she finds that not only was their closeness compatible with their celibate dedication but they lived all the virtues with heroic perfection. Their friendships furthered their total commitment to God and to all of his people.

Yet the story cannot end at this point. Not every closeness to other human persons is compatible with a complete self-gift to the Lord. What used to be called "particular friendships" are a bane to religious communities because they are exclusive, self-seeking, clique-forming, and time-absorbing. *They* indeed are opposed to the universality that is to characterize the virginal way of loving. And it goes without saying that friendships that tend to the romantic and to the erotic are entirely inimical to this evangelical life. They not only sterilize a serious prayer life, but they only too often scandalize the faithful and lead to a serious violation of publicly taken vows. The special friendship of which we speak here has nothing to do with these shabby imitations of romance and marriage. We may characterize in positive terms just what it does entail.

Authentic celibate friendship is thoroughly immersed in God. Not only does it begin in a common religious concern (for example, a priest and a sister working in the same parish), but it continues throughout in that total immersion. God so remains the chief concern of both parties that they would not offend him deliberately in the least way, not only as regards their vows but in any way. Celibate friendship of this mature type is not therefore likely in very young people, for it supposes a deepening prayer life in both individuals, whether they be of the same sex or not. It is this depth in God that accounts for the other traits of which we shall be speaking, and it makes clear that we are not dealing with a mere need relationship. Human beings cannot be deep with one another unless they are individually deep as persons. Genuine closeness does not happen simply because two people wish it to happen. It is because the ingredients are already there that the saints are capable of profound, warm, selfless relationships that far transcend the level of meeting one's own needs—even though it is true that needs are also met.

The second trait of special friendship is that it furthers celibate dedication. If a priest and religious begin seriously to think of marriage and the consequent dispensation from vows, they may be sure that their attraction is no longer (if ever it was) a love given by the Holy Spirit. The reason they may be sure is that God does not first give the permanent celibate charism and then proceed to chip away at it. The virginal gift and genuine human love, because they are given by the same Spirit, will reinforce each other. Close friendships among the saints strengthen them in their resolve; they want their consecration more, not less.

Third, the friendship is non-exclusive, non-possessive. Each friend is pleased that the other has other close relationships. While it is right, indeed imperative, that a wife love her husband exclusively and possessively (and he, her), the celibate man or woman does not give another marital attention—that is reserved for the Lord alone.

Saint Paul calls it undivided. This trait therefore makes it entirely possible for religious to love another deeply and yet treat others with the equal concern the Apostle requires in Christian community (Rom 12:16). Completely excluded is the immature relationship religious used to criticize under the caption of "particular friendship".

Virginal friendship not only is compatible with community life but it also increases the very universality that is one of its essential traits. The vowed person loves individuals, of course (we do not love abstract human nature or society as a generality), and in responding to each one's unique gifts finds that he is growing in love even for those to whom he is not especially close. It is after all the same virtue of charity by which we love our close friends and all others. These different loves grow or languish together, for God is the reason for anyone's lovableness.

Fifth, the celibate friendship of the saints deepens prayer life and commitment to it. The reason is the same as what we have just mentioned: the love by which we love our dear friends is the same as that which is the core of our prayer—they grow together or they die together.

Finally, celibate friends are not excessive in the amount of time they spend in each other's company. What exactly is unreasonable attention cannot be spelled out with one hard and fast rule, but we may say that if the other five traits are present, each friend will readily know what is due and proper in the concrete circumstances. If the two friends live under the same roof (for example, two religious in the same house), there may be occasions for special sharing, but on the whole they will give as much time and attention to other members of the community as to the special friend. This, after all, is simply fulfilling the Pauline injunction that Christians treat everyone with equal kindness.

From all of the above it follows that there is no place for a quasi-romantic "third way" between marital love and faithful virginal love. A great deal of scandal (not to mention outright violation of vows) has been given in recent decades by celibate men and women naïvely engaging in inappropriate marks of affection and in dating. While we do find warmth and demonstrated affection among the saints, we emphatically do *not* find a courting relationship. Prayerful people know the difference.

Virginity Leads to Deepening Human Love

We now proceed a step further. The celibate charism is not only compatible with warm human love, it brings this love into being and carries it into new depths. Not only may the consecrated person learn to love other human persons in a generous, cordial warmth—he grows in this warmth to the extent that he lives his virginal gift. This is a strong statement and it needs strong proof. We have in this claim an example of the divine assertion that God's thoughts are not ours, that as the heavens are above the earth, so his thoughts transcend ours (Is 55:8–9). Reluctant as the world is to believe this claim, outrageous as it is to secular ears, anyone who has experienced the love of a deeply prayerful religious knows it to be true.

To see why virginity promotes genuine human love we need only recall that a profound contemplative communion is the primary reason for the consecration. In the very nature of things, one who has achieved this purpose has necessarily achieved also a warm love for neighbor. Deepening contemplation makes one sensitive to beauty, created and uncreated. As the wise man remarked, God puts his own light into prayerful hearts "to show them the magnificence of his works" (Sir 17:7–8). The contemplative sees more beauty in fellow human beings because he has the enabling divine light. He consequently finds it much easier to love others. When we read that Saint Francis of Assisi kissed a leper, we ought not to conclude that the saint found leprosy attractive. He found the leper attractive. Because Francis was a mystic, he saw a beauty in the disfigured body that most of us cannot see. Paul is of a like mind even when he finds it necessary to correct the wayward: "When I wrote to you, in deep distress and anguish of mind and in tears, it was not to make you feel hurt but to let you know how much love I have for you" (2 Cor 2:4).

The primary celibate orientation to deep prayer, to undivided attention to the Lord, is necessarily an orientation to warm human love, since the love of God cannot be separated from the love of one's sisters and brothers. As John the Evangelist put it, a person who does not love the brother whom he sees cannot love the God whom he does not see (1 Jn 4:20). As love for God increases in prayer it must increase in daily activities as well. Catherine deHueck Doherty has noted that in silent prayer "availability will become delightsome and easy, for in each person the soul will see the face of her Love. Hospitality will be deep and real, for a silent heart is a loving heart, and a loving heart is a hospice to the world" (*Poustinia*, p. 21).

As prayer develops, one progressively puts on the mind of God, and consequently sees his fellows as God does, as "precious in my eyes", as "God's beloved" (Is 43:4; Rom 1:7). Loving becomes much easier and much warmer, indeed even tender, because one sees with new eyes, divinized eyes. This is why Paul saw his people as sacred and holy (1 Cor 3:16–17) and as being transformed from one beauty to another (2 Cor 3:18). Because God loves us far beyond our wildest imagination, the virgin's prayerful lifestyle slowly enables her to love others as he does. Her undivided attention to him gradually clothes her mind and heart with his.

Apostolic Availability

> It is not ourselves that we are preaching but Christ Jesus.
>
> (2 Corinthians 4:5)

By this time the reader has probably noticed something that would strike many people as odd. If the general population sees a value in celibate dedication, that value is in benefiting the human family through teaching, nursing, or social service. Yet thus far we have said little about the relationship between virginity and service. What we have said is what most people do *not* think about when they consider consecrated chastity. Yet in God's thought it is primary, and that is why we have placed the emphasis on prayer and love.

Yet service is important. It is not primary, but nonetheless it remains an important element in the lives of many who embrace gospel virginity as a way of life. God calls some to this radical surrender for the sake of prayer alone. Most of these enter a cloistered community, though there is a growing movement to hermit life as well. He calls others to prayer and apostolic endeavor. To these latter we now turn direct attention, that is, to the work aspect of their lives.

The New Testament does not explicitly mention apostolate as a reason for dedicated chastity. The reason explicitly given is freedom for undivided attention to the person of the Lord and for his kingdom, a kingdom that he describes as within us. Yet the New Testament does implicitly suggest that celibacy is oriented secondarily to apostolic work. When certain people are said to give up marriage, it is for the sake of the gospel, the kingdom (Mk 10:28–30; Lk 18:29–30). Saint Paul teaches that the virgin is to be concerned with the things of the Lord, and surely one of his "things" is the work of spreading his word and healing with his sacraments.

The virginal lifestyle is obviously suited to complete freedom for apostolic commitment. The celibate person is freed from the limitations of family life, from the hundred concerns involved with caring for a husband or wife and children. There is a wideness, an openness in both the availability of time and of warm love. Like the celibate Saint Paul, the virgin can, if and when necessary, roam from one end of an empire to the other in proclaiming the words and deeds of the Lord Jesus.

Further along it shall become clear that prayer and apostolate are by no means to be set in opposition. For those called to proclamation and other forms of service, prayer and work are either found together or they separately wither. We are not Pelagians. Professional competency is important, but of itself it brings no one to God. The apostle is supernaturally effective precisely to the degree that he has a deep relationship with the Lord of grace. "Without me you can do nothing" (Jn 15:5; cf. 14:6).

CHAPTER EIGHT

WHO IS A CONSECRATED WOMAN?

The Gospel concept of virginity is so rich a reality it cannot be described in a paragraph or a page. Even though we have now devoted a number of pages to our subject, we have not yet set it into an adequate context, the context of the divine economy of salvation, the people of God, the *ekklesia*. To see this wider picture we shall sketch a mosaic, and just as with any mosaic, we do not get the whole message until we perceive each of the stones and how together they make a totality. Beauty is a splendor of truth radiant in a lovely form, one in which each part contributes to the fascination of the whole. It takes many petals to make a rose and thousands of leaves to produce a tree.

The virgin must be seen in the midst of God's people, for she is not an isolated figure cut off from the business of life. She seeks solitude, yes, but her type of solitude is light years from isolation. In each of our mosaic-answers to the question "Who is a consecrated woman?" we shall note how she relates to the whole Church. She is eminently an ecclesial woman with an ecclesial charism.

Woman of the word–Word

> Let the word of Christ in all its richness find a home with you.
>
> (Colossians 3:16)

God's word is powerful, dramatic. It is like fire and a hammer breaking rocks (Jer 23:29). It is a two-edged sword that cuts, pierces, divides, discerns (Heb 4:12). It transforms, heals, and beautifies. When we say that the virgin is a woman of the word, we are saying nothing dull, prosaic, or weak. She heals, transforms, and beautifies.

By his word spoken into the world, God gathers a people to himself. In the old dispensation he spoke in diverse ways through the prophets. In the new age he has spoken the final, unsurpassable word in his Son, the incarnate Word. By this last intervention he has gathered his new people together, close to himself and close to one another. The virgin gathers people to the Lord and close to their brothers and sisters. In a new sense the virgin is a sister among siblings.

All God's people are to ponder his message in prayerful reflection. That man is blessed who meditates the divine word day and night (Ps 1:1–2). When the Lord's message penetrates to the marrow of our bones, we are slowly healed, transformed into the very image that we reflect (2 Cor 3:18).

Celibacy affords a double freedom in regard to God's word. This lifestyle liberates one to ponder the divine proclamation at greater length and with less distraction. Saint Luke twice tells us that the first consecrated virgin, the Mother of Jesus, was characterized by her inner pondering of the holy happenings she had experienced (Lk 2:19, 51). Jesus commends as the one thing, the prime necessity of human life, this undivided attending to his person and his message (Lk 10:38–42).

When she is called to engage in apostolic work, the virgin's way of life affords her a freedom for unimpeded involvement in serving others. Because she is concerned neither with looking after a husband and children nor with the distractions of fine clothing, elegant dining, and expensive recreations, she is at liberty to love others unstintingly and to aid them accordingly. Both her life and her speech are words that proclaim the Word.

Prophetic Woman

> There was a prophetess . . . serving God night and day with fasting and prayer.
>
> (Luke 2:36–37).

A biblical prophet is a charismatic man or woman called and sent by the Lord to proclaim his holy will by deed and by word. As charismatic, the prophet is gifted for the community, not just for himself. God takes the initiative and commissions him for his task. A prophet is not an innovator; he proclaims the undiluted will of the Lord God in a life and word of burning zeal.

The virgin is charismatic because she is gifted for the community. The primary prayer orientation of her virginity is a gift to the Church at large because we keenly need certain people so to live that they can *be* prayer in the midst of the Church. The dedicated woman is needed, not simply to pray for the wants and woundedness of our world, but to be prayer within it. She is needed to live in the flesh fully and obviously what the Church herself is, a society of prayer.

The consecrated person is charismatic because her factual frugality is a living witness to the sparing-sharing manner of life all God's people must live. "If anyone has two tunics he must share with the man who has none", we read, "and the one with something to eat must do the same" (Lk 3:10). No one who does not share his wealth with his needy brother can love God (1 Jn 3:17–18). The virgin's simple lifestyle is a witness to the world of what all must do: share with the poor.

She is prophetic because she is radical. Unafraid to challenge conventional wisdom, she proclaims in her life that God's thoughts and ways are not ours. She chooses to be countercultural, a nonconformist in the best sense of the term. Like Saint

Paul she proclaims in life and word the undiluted word of God (2 Cor 4:2).

Like all the prophets, this woman works within her tradition and is faithful to it. Like Catherine of Siena she may speak up to leaders, but her word of praise or of censure springs from a love both for the authorities and for the community committed to them. Knowing nothing of a shrill hostility, she clings to the leader's teaching (Acts 2:42), to sound doctrine (1 Tim 4:6; Titus 1:9). She is faithful to the Lord of the Church who called her to follow in his footsteps.

What does the virgin proclaim in life and word? Many things. One is that God is her first choice. He is more than first (for any person God must be first)—he is the *only* center of her being. Her life says "With my whole heart I seek you" (Ps 119:10). Her eyes are always on the Lord (Ps 25:15). She proclaims also a freedom from the many conformisms in our world, from the tyrannies of social prestige, sexual domination, and financial power seeking. She proclaims the humility without which one neither understands God nor enters into his kingdom. She asserts an active love for sister and brother in a sparing-sharing mode of life. Like the Mother of the Lord she heralds the joy of her virginity (Lk 1:46–47).

Free Woman

> If the Son makes you free, you will be free indeed.
> (John 8:36).

Most people are persuaded that freedom is mainly an immunity from laws, regulations, restrictions. It does imply this immunity to some extent, but before all else freedom is a positive power to be and to do. Even if there are no restrictions at all, I am not free to play the piano unless I possess the knowledge, capacities, and abilities that will enable me to play. A doctor is not free to heal simply because no one is physically restraining him. He is free to be a doctor only when he possesses the various skills and knowledge needed in his profession. We are free in Christ because he gives us the powers to be a new creation, a transformed human being. Without these powers we are forever slaves to our selfishness, pride, lust, vanity, laziness, and all else.

Further, you and I are free only to the extent that we want to do what we do. If you go to a party, give a gift, or work at your job because of social pressure or external force (that is, you really do not want to do what you do), you are acting in a slavish manner. We are supremely emancipated when we fully desire to work, play, pray, and all else. Because the Holy Spirit gives us the very desire and will to do the fully human thing, he rids us of our operating under pressures, against our will, in a servile manner.

In her chaste and frugal life, the dedicated person more easily attains this enlarging liberation. The first word Saint Paul says about virginal dedication is a word about release: "I would have you free from care" (1 Cor 7:32). When she vows a voluntary poverty (and keeps the vow), she is disentangled from being possessed by mere things. "If anyone lets himself be dominated by anything, then he is a slave to it" (2 Pet 2:19). She is extricated from the rigid neo-conformism of style, position, prestige. She is cut loose from the shallowness, the hollowness of a tinsel world, and thus she is enabled, with Paul, to have nothing and yet to possess all things (2 Cor 6:10). She is unshackled from seeking a false sense of security in this world. She knows that fine clothing, beautiful furniture, luxurious jewelry offer no assurance at all against the ravages of illness, aging, and eventual death. She has accepted the word of Jesus: "Watch, and be on your guard against avarice of any kind, for a man's life is not made secure by what he owns, even when he has more than he needs" (Lk 12:15).

This woman is unfettered from the limitations, even the worthy limitations, of family life. Good as it is, marriage is so confining that many people today avoid it for purely selfish reasons. When it is given up for generous purposes, the autonomy universalizes love and concern.

Frugal celibacy enables one to be a healthy (not a negative, carping) critic of society, free to challenge its ideological assumptions. This person can easily speak out against the self-centered promises of "the good life", of proprietary interests, of the absolutizing of pleasure and sexuality.

The celibate is especially liberated for a prayer-centered lifestyle. This is so crucial a sovereignty that we shall have to return to it explicitly and at length further on.

Woman in Love

> My spirit rejoices in God my savior.
>
> (Luke 1:47)

The Christian virgin is a woman in love. I do not say simply a woman of love. That, yes; but more. Because her heart has been captured by her Beloved, in at least a beginning manner, she is absorbed in him. As Paul puts it, she is not concerned with the world and its business, but with the affairs of the Lord. As anyone really in love does, she gives her undivided attention to him (1 Cor 7:34–35).

To be in love means to be head over heels in love. It is a state in which everything is the same and yet nothing is the same. For as long as the smitten state lasts reality is transformed. Virginity aims at living fully the being-in-love Scripture everywhere supposes: "My eyes are always on the Lord . . . my soul yearns for you in the night . . . ah, you are beautiful, my beloved . . . with my whole heart I seek you . . . sing to the Lord in your hearts always and everywhere . . ." (Ps 25:15; Is 26:9; Song 4:1; Ps 119:10; Eph 5:20). This is why the virgin puts prayer first in her life. She is in love with God and with his people.

Woman of Prayer

> I am going to lure her and lead her out into the wilderness and speak to her heart.
>
> (Hosea 2:16)

God calls all men and women of whatever vocation to a deep communion with himself. He invites everyone to a prayer so profound that one becomes radiant with joy; the person tastes and sees for himself how good he is (Ps 34:5, 8). He wants everyone to hunger and thirst for him (Ps 63:1), to pant after his word (Ps 119:131), to meditate on his message day and night (Ps 1:1–2), to rejoice in him always (Phil 4:4), to experience a joy in him so amazing that it cannot be described (1 Pet 1:8), to pray continually, all day long (Lk 18:1; Ps 84:4).

Scripture calls this prayerful immersion in God

the one thing, the main business of the human enterprise. The one thing we ask of the Lord, the one thing we seek is to gaze on his beauty and contemplate his temple (Ps 27:4). A prayerful listening to his word is the prime necessity in human life (Lk 10:38–42). This is so because it is prayer and pondering God's word that transforms us to full personal beauty.

Because she is literally in love, the consecrated woman is before all else a woman of prayer. Like Jesus himself she is drawn irresistibly to long, frequent times of solitude with the Father. Anyone in love desires to commune long and lovingly with the beloved. No one has to urge her to it. The authentic celibate readily understands why the Second Vatican Council declared that religious are in a diocese not primarily for apostolic work but for prayer, penance, and example (CD, 33). She can see why, in the Church, action is subordinated to contemplation (SC, 2). She grasps easily why even apostolic religious are presumed by the Council to be "thoroughly enriched with the treasures of mysticism" (AGD, 18). The new Code of Canon Law summarizes this primary orientation of celibacy in one sentence: "The contemplation of divine things and an assiduous union with God in prayer is to be the first and principal duty of all religious" (Canon 663, §1).

We can put the matter in another way: a woman embraces virginity primarily so that she may more

easily experience what the mystics wrote about.
And what did they write about?—A breathlessly
beautiful love affair with God, a prayerful enthrallment in him, a being lost in love, immersed in it.
Let me offer just one example among many possible. Incomparable Saint Augustine, a man who
had experienced the lowest and the loftiest of
human delights, addresses himself to God after
his conversion:

> Too late have I loved you, O Beauty so ancient
> and so new, too late have I loved you. . . . You
> have sent forth fragrance, and I have drawn in
> my breath, and I pant after you. I have tasted
> you, and I hunger and thirst after you. You have
> touched me, and I have burned for your peace.
> . . . My life will be life indeed, filled wholly with
> you. . . . Sometimes you admit me in my inner-
> most being into a most extraordinary affection,
> mounting within me to an indescribable delight.
> If this is perfected in me, it will be something, I
> know not what, that will not belong to this life.[1]

The virgin is one who wishes a lifestyle tailor-
made so that she may more readily attain that life
of prayer to which Augustine refers, so that she
may be "already filled with a joy so glorious that
it cannot be described" (1 Pet 1:8).

[1] Saint Augustine, *Confessions,* trans. John K. Ryan (New
York: Doubleday, Image edition, 1960), book 10, chapters
27 and 40, pp. 254–255, 272.

Poor Pilgrim

> We brought nothing into the world and we can
> take nothing out of it, but as long as we have
> food and clothing, let us be content with that.
> (1 Timothy 1:7–8)

All of God's people are pilgrims, strangers to this world, nomads on the face of the earth (Heb 11:13–16). We have here no lasting city. We are traveling to our resting place, the heavenly homeland where, risen with Christ Jesus, we shall rejoice with him forever (Phil 3:20–21).

Pilgrims, as distinguished from pleasure travelers, travel lightly. We brought nothing into the world and we shall leave it with nothing. We are thus content with the bare necessities of life. We are free, detached. We are not to worry about what we eat, drink, and wear. The pagans who know not that they are nomads worry about these things, but we are to set our hearts on the kingdom, our destination (Mt 6:31–33). Sojourners on the way to the sacred shrine gladly share their goods with their companions. They live a sparing-sharing travel style because their hearts are set, not on the passing journey, but on the destination.

Scripture relates virginity to frugality. In one breath Luke speaks of those who give up their property for the kingdom as also giving up marriage (Lk 18:29–30). The celibate Paul writes of the virgin as being concerned, not with the affairs of the world, but with those of the Lord. He describes himself as possessing nothing (2 Cor 6:10). The virgin follows the celibate, poor Christ and with him reaps the rich fulfillment reserved for those who hunger for what is right and holy.

The consecrated woman is to all women a model of putting first things first. She is not preoccupied with outer adornment, fine clothes, jewelry (1 Tim 2:9). She is well disposed for contemplation because she is uncluttered with mere things. She can think as the poor think in her choices: recreating, eating, drinking, traveling, gift giving. She does not merely say pious words about aiding the poor. She loves them as herself in deed as well as in word. Rather than buy, make, or receive a dress for herself, she will buy, make, or receive it for some poor woman in the third world who has none. She appears authentic to others because she *is* authentic.

Woman of the Church

> The virgin is concerned with the things of the Lord.
>
> (1 Corinthians 7:34)

Every baptized person is necessarily a man or woman of the Church, for baptism is the sacrament of rebirth and incorporation into the mystical Christ. When we speak of the Christian virgin as a woman of the Church, we mean that her consecration, rooted deeply as it is in baptism, is a new and unique living of what the Church is. We can even say that she is, in her dedication, the Church concentrated.

What does this mean? The New Testament places the life of consecrated chastity in an ecclesial context. We read that those who leave property, family, and marriage do so for the kingdom, not only for their own advantage. Saint Paul regards the virgin as concerned with the Lord's affairs, not just her private growth. Because of her femininity, the virgin can *be* and *image* the Church in two ways that men cannot share—at least not fully.

The first of these is that she lives and images the Church's wedded intimacy with her Lord. Scripture again and again speaks of the wedding between God and his bride, the *ekklesia*. This image is meant to bring out the profound love-communion he wishes with his people: ideal marriage illustrates it. We read that "Yahweh takes delight in you and your land will have its wedding. Like a young man marrying a virgin, so will the one who built you wed you, and as the bride-groom rejoices in his bride, so will your God rejoice in you" (Is 62:4–5). When his bride is unfaithful, this God still continues to woo her back: "I am going to lure her into the wilderness and speak to her heart" (Hos 2:16). Saint Paul applies this theme to the Church of the New Testament: "You see the jealousy that I feel for you is God's own jealousy: I arranged for you to marry Christ so that I might give you away as a chaste virgin to this one husband" (2 Cor 11:2). We have already noted that the Apostle considers the individual consecrated virgin to be wedded to Christ in a special manner and that Saint Ambrose, writing in the fourth century, captured this idea in five words: *"Virgo est quae Deo nubit"* (a virgin is a woman who has married God). This formulation well expresses what is implied in the life of complete chastity: exclusive, total love, intimacy of intercommunion, unreserved self-gift, unending fidelity, service to the beloved, mutual delight. This is why to this day the liturgy for the profession of religious women continues to give prominence to the bridal theme. Profession day is a wedding day. The virginal gift is an ecclesial charism. This woman is the Church concentrated.

Second, she is uniquely the woman of the Church in still another way: she lives and images the Church's motherhood. If a man, Saint Paul, can speak of himself as begetting new life through God's word (1 Cor 4:15), we can speak of a woman of the word as begetting new life. If Paul may see himself as a father, the virgin may consider herself a mother. Vatican Council II spoke of celibacy as "a unique fountain of spiritual fertility in the world" (LG, 42). The consecrated woman shares in this ecclesial motherhood.

This she does in three ways: prayer-love, works of service, and sacrificial giving. Speaking of cloistered religious, Pope Pius XI could write, "It is these very pure and lofty souls who, by their love, their suffering, and their prayers, exercise in silence within the Church the apostolate which is the most universal and the most fruitful." Just as the hierarchical element in the *ekklesia* must itself first pray and then proclaim the word (Acts 6:3–4), so the dedicated woman prays and then serves. Because her consecration is oriented to prayerful love before all else, she enjoys a primacy of motherhood. Her being prayer within the Church is "the most universal and the most fruitful" apostolate. She is consequently the most universal and fruitful mother in the midst of God's people.

She is lifegiving in her work as well. In the fourth century, Gregory of Nyssa expressed this idea lucidly: "Truly and solidly does the virgin mother rejoice, for she by her spiritual work gives birth to immortal children." Anyone who begets love begets life. And this is the function of the consecrated woman.

Finally, she is mother in her sacrificial self-gift. Jesus could affirm that "unless a wheat grain falls on the ground and dies, it remains only a single grain; but if it dies, it yields a rich harvest" (Jn

12:24). By her radical self-donation the virgin pilgrim enters more deeply into the life-bringing Passion of Christ and is thus, with him, renewing the face of the earth, bringing it to new life.

The existence to which the celibate woman gives birth from the womb of the Church surpasses natural life as heaven surpasses earth. As the liturgy for Holy Saturday sings, what would it profit us to be born the first time if we had not been reborn a second time? The virgin's motherliness penetrates into the order of final enthrallment in risen body. (She begets bodily life in this sense.) Her fecundity knows no bereavement, no disturbance of the flesh, no division of the heart, no distractions at prayer. It spans oceans and continents. She is on this score also the Church concentrated.

Image of Mary

> A great sign appeared in heaven: a woman, adorned with the sun, standing on the moon, and with the twelve stars on her head for a crown.
>
> (Revelation 12:1)

Because she is ecclesial, the virgin is also Marian. She is to remind all the faithful of the Mother of the Lord Jesus. Only a woman can recall us fully to the greatest of all women. In his exhortation to religious Pope Paul VI could say: "Would that your life, patterned after her [Mary's] example, might witness to that motherly love by which all should be animated who cooperate in the Church's apostolic mission of regenerating mankind." Only a virgin can remind us of her who combined in her person the two feminine glories of virginity and motherhood.

The consecrated woman is Marian in other ways as well. She is a woman wrapped up in Jesus, a woman who ponders the Word day and night, a radical, prophetic, total woman, a woman of prayer and love, a universal mother.

Reflection of Deepest Feminine Beauty

> Do not dress up for show: doing up your hair, wearing gold bracelets and fine clothes; all this should be inside, in a person's heart, imperishable: the ornament of a sweet and gentle disposition— this is what is precious in God's sight. That was how the holy women of the past dressed themselves attractively.
>
> (1 Peter 3:3–5)

Scripture speaks more than once of feminine beauty. Ezekiel refers to God's people (his spouse) as being given a queenly beauty, perfect and famous (Ezek 16:13–14). The Song of Songs speaks of the bride as being beloved, beautiful, sweet, lovely. Judith is said to be "beautifully formed

and lovely to behold—a very God-fearing woman" (Judith 8:7–8). The most important aspect of feminine charm, however, is the radiance
of inner goodness. In the new creation women
are so to attract others from inner innocence and
sanctity that they need not depend on outer adornment, fine clothing, golden jewelry (see also 1
Tim 2:9).

Because her Beloved dwells within her heart,
the virgin is not out to catch the eyes of men. She
is not trying to impress and win a future husband
or to retain a present one. She more easily can
remind all, men and women alike, of what is most
beautiful in a woman: love, fidelity, innocence,
gentleness. She proclaims with her being what is
most precious in the sight of God.

Figure of Final Fulfillment

> Our present perishable nature must put on imper-
> ishability and this mortal nature must put on im-
> mortality.
>
> (1 Cor 15:53)

If the consecrated woman reminds the world that
womanly comeliness is not primarily a transitory
physical form, she also proclaims that a woman
is not a mere thing, a simple means to male pleasure. The virgin declares in her being that woman
has an independent personal dignity that trans-

cends the fleeting allurements of a body destined
to the disfigurement and dissolution of aging, illness, and death. She proclaims that final bodily
splendor will be the lot of the virtuous when they
reign with Christ in the glory of their risen bodies.

One with the virginal charism anticipates the
final completion. She gives up in the bloom of
youth what everyone gives up at the moment of
death. The millionaire owns not a penny as he
breathes his last. He is no longer married. He no
longer freely disposes of himself even in the wiggle
of a finger. The virgin lives the paschal emptying
from her youth and she derives a reward "many
times over even in this present time" (Lk 18:29–
30).

Woman of Totality

> Christ Jesus never wavered between Yes and No.
> With him it was always Yes.
>
> (2 Corinthians 1:19)

Our sketch of who the virgin is could be sum-
marized in several ways. Our last caption, totality,
is one of them. Most people are at home with the
average, the mediocre. They fear wholeness, totality, as a threat—while actually it is a compliment.
God is never a God of fractions. He always asks
everything. He does not say, "Love the Lord your
God with most of your heart", but with *all* of it

(Mt 22:37). He does not require us to be more or less merciful, but to "be perfect as your heavenly Father is perfect" (Mt 5:48). He does not say pray often, but continually, always and everywhere (Lk 18:1; Eph 5:19–20). All of this is a compliment to the human person. We are so great, our potentialities are so grand, that we must aspire, not to the middling, but to the perfect; not to the partial, but to the full.

The biblical sketch of radical dedication is always a sketch of totality. The virgin is to give undivided attention to the Lord, to keep her eyes always on her God, to live the whole revealed word, poverty and celibacy included, to be universally available to her sisters and brothers, to love with universal warmth, to be both virgin and mother. Like the Lord Jesus himself, she is not one to waver between Yes and No. With her it must be always Yes.

CHAPTER NINE

AN INTEGRATED LIFESTYLE

A divinely-originated way of life makes sense. Young people would say that it hangs together. Because consecrated virginity is a valid vocation, it must possess an inner coherence. As a valid way of living it must present a consuming goal together with a consistent mode of life that leads to that goal. As a matter of fact, in the present-day Church there is not just one way to live consecrated chastity; there are several. We shall summarize each briefly.

Private Dedication

In the history of the Catholic Church the first manner in which women pledged their chastity to Christ was in private consecration. Though they dwelt in their own homes, they lived their exclusive love for him in an individual manner. They did not join religious communities because there were none to join. Still a live option in the contemporary Church, this type of dedication comes about when a person makes a private vow of chastity or virginity. She (he) may add vows of poverty and obedience according to a specified rule and under the guidance of a spiritual director. This consecration is non-canonical because there is no special relationship with the bishop of the locality.

Hermit Life

Although one may live perfect chastity privately either in complete solitude or in the midst of a busy city, there is also the option of embracing a canonical eremitic life, that is, one recognized in canon law, with the approval and under the direction of a bishop. Canon 603 speaks of this now officially recognized state:

§1. Besides institutes of consecrated life, the Church recognizes the eremitic or anchoritic life by which the Christian faithful devote their life to the praise of God and salvation of the world through a stricter separation from the world, the silence of solitude and assiduous prayer and penance.

§2. A hermit is recognized in the law as one dedicated to God in a consecrated life if he or she publicly professes the three evangelical counsels, confirmed by a vow or other sacred bond, in the hands of the diocesan bishop and observes his or her own plan of life under his direction.[1]

The canonical hermit does well to have a written rule and an immediate *abba* or superior, approved by the bishop, to whom she (he) has recourse for guidance and for routine permissions. This hermit may find solitude either in a rural area or in the midst of a busy city.

Order of Virgins

Hearkening back to the early centuries of Church history, the new code provides also for unmarried women who under the inspiration of the Holy Spirit wish, with or without vows, to consecrate their chastity to Christ:

> Canon 604, §1. Similar to these forms of consecrated life is the order of virgins, who, committed to the holy plan of following Christ more closely, are consecrated to God by the diocesan bishop according to the approved liturgical rite, are betrothed mystically to Christ, the Son of God, and are dedicated to the service of the Church.

[1] The translation is that approved in 1983 by the National Conference of Catholic Bishops in the United States.

§2. In order to observe their commitment more faithfully and to perform by mutual support service to the Church which is in harmony with their state these virgins can form themselves into associations.

It should be noted that the Church in accord with our whole tradition sees this consecration in marital terms. The new ritual which has revised the older rite of consecration lays down the following requirements:

a. These women "should always have been unmarried, and never lived in public or open violation of chastity;

b. "By their age, prudence, and universally approved character they should give assurance of perseverance in a life of chastity dedicated to the service of the Church and of their neighbor;

c. "They should be admitted to the consecration by the bishop who is ordinary of the place."[2]

Secular Institutes

This manner of evangelical consecration is a vowed and organized living in the world of the three evangelical counsels of celibacy, obedience,

[2] *The Code of Canon Law: A Text and Commentary,* edited by James A. Coriden, Thomas J. Green, and Donald E. Heintschel (New York: Paulist Press, 1985), p. 468.

and poverty. Members of these institutes live a professedly secular life in the world, while at the same time they possess a new freedom for prayer. They retain their ordinary employment and they wear no religious garb. They usually live alone or with their families and meet occasionally with fellow members. Neither their witness nor their apostolate is corporate. They bring a gospel spirit into the world through their hidden presence. The norms governing this form of consecration are found in canons 710 to 730.

Active Religious Institutes

This most common and familiar way of living celibacy is an organized and communal living of the three counsels under vows and in a non-secular lifestyle. Members give a gospel witness through a visible community life and a corporate apostolate. To prayer, their main concern, they join differing types of ecclesial work. Like members of secular institutes, religious live according to a rule and under the direction of leadership. Unlike the former, they are not hidden in the world but visibly differ from the world both in manner of communal life and in dress.

Societies of Apostolic Life

Members of these institutes do not take religious vows but they do perform apostolic work and live in community according to a special way of life expressed in their constitutions. Some of these societies have their members assume the three evangelical counsels by bonds (other than vows) defined in their constitutions (Canon 731).

Cloistered Religious Orders

Enclosed life is the most radical of the communal ways of living the three gospel counsels. These institutes share much in common with active ones. They differ chiefly in that they do not have an external apostolate but rather are oriented wholly to prayer, solitude, and penance. Their work is limited to the care of the monastery and their own needs together with some income-producing activities that can be carried on within the enclosure. Members are assured of the freedom for prayerful solitude by the practice of enclosure, which limits their contacts with persons in the outside world.

Whatever the precise manner of life, an integrated gospel pattern requires the harmonious interweaving of prayer, work, recreation, and rest. In each of the types mentioned, these four elements are mingled in various ways. In all of them, however, prayer is the prime necessity. Why this is so is the subject of our next section. No state of life may contradict the gospel message, and for the revealed word, communing with the Lord God is the overriding necessity of all human existence.

CHAPTER TEN

PRAYER/LOVE

We will continue to devote ourselves to prayer
and to the service of the word.

(Acts 6:4)

No one makes it in life unless he possesses a deep,
exclusive love. By "makes it in life" I do not mean
simply surviving. Anyone can *survive* without
love. By "makes it in life" I mean reaching a full-
ness-of-person beauty and happiness. By "deep,
exclusive love" I do not refer to any merely human
love, not even the love found in an ideal marriage.
No merely natural relationship is the ultimate answer to the human puzzle. By "deep, exclusive
love" I refer to a love that is given to one alone
and with no reservations whatsoever. That kind
of love can be had for God only.

Prayer is the overriding necessity, the biblical
"one thing necessary", for any human person.
Vatican Council II was on target in affirming that
in the Church, action is subordinated to contemplation. We have said above that, both for Saint
Paul and for the contemporary teaching Church,

the primary reason for virginity is a freedom for prayer and love. The Christian virgin gives up a marital relationship with a mere man in order to enjoy more freedom to develop a profound intimacy with God, to focus on the things of the Lord, to give him undivided attention (1 Cor 7:34–35).

Because drinking from the divine Fountain is the only genuine fulfillment, the virgin puts prayer in the primary place in her life. She drinks joy from the waters of salvation. She tastes and sees for herself how good the Lord is (Ps 34:8).

But there are other reasons, too, for the primacy of prayer. Neither the celibate nor anyone else will live the gospel fully without deep prayer. No one can live without pleasure. The difference between sinner and saint is not that the former has his pleasures while the latter does not. Quite the contrary. While the sinner experiences brief, paltry pleasures, the saint drinks a continual delight that the sinner cannot even suspect. The sinner experiences frequent basic disappointments, even bitterness. While the saint is not exempt from suffering and ordinary human disappointments, he experiences nothing of the sinner's bitterness and disillusionment. God draws men and women from their petty selfishnesses (detractions, vanity, coldness, deceit, impatience) by giving them a liberating joy. This delight frees them from seek-

woman. Like Mary, the first consecrated virgin, she ponders the word in her heart. She is before all else a woman wrapped in an absorbing concern for her Beloved.

CHAPTER ELEVEN

VIRGINITY AND TOTALITY

Even on the natural level of creation, familiarity for most of us begets dullness. We have seen so many trees that the miracle of an acorn developing into a majestic oak leaves us unimpressed. We do not wonder that grass can bend in the breeze and yet not break. Almost no one marvels at the unfathomable atoms in a speck of dust. We have just considered the "much more" resulting from generously lived celibacy, and the reader can test his own response: "Am I struck with amazement at the idea?" Probably not.

Likely enough most writers on the subject are not struck either, for we seldom if ever read of any development of what this hundredfold may include. Biblical writers are surely impressed with God's gifts, but we have read and heard their proclamations so often that they leave little or no mark on our consciousness: "I have come that they may have life and have it abundantly . . . [we are] to be filled with the utter fullness of God . . . transformed from one glory to another . . . we shall be like him . . . much more in this present time and in addition life everlasting . . . eye has not

seen, nor ear heard . . ." (Jn 10:10; Eph 3:19; 2 Cor
3:18; 1 Jn 3:2; Lk 18:29–30; 1 Cor 2:9). The same
non-reaction greets statements of the teaching
Church. Vatican Council II said dozens of splendid
things about our destiny, about contemplation,
about virginity, and we have seen it submerged by
popularizers as they saw in the Council what they
wanted to see and only too often what was not there.

Hence we shall try to overcome our dullness
by seeing the "utter fullness of God" and the hundredfold where indeed they must be perceived,
namely, in the depths of communion with the
triune God as they are described by Saints John
of the Cross and Teresa of Avila. A comprehensive
treatment of the transforming union must wait
for another volume, and so here we shall make
two points briefly. The first is that all men and
women are called to this utter fullness of God,
and the second that the primary purpose of virginity is a readier path to it.

The mind of Saint Paul is clear. He wants all
the Corinthians now in this life to be transformed
from "one glory to another into the image" of
God himself (2 Cor 3:18). What the apostle has
in mind is so unspeakable a transformation in love
that no eye has seen, no ear has heard anything
comparable, nor can it dawn on our imagination
what God has prepared even in this life for those
who love as they ought. What John and Teresa
describe cannot be more than this "utter fullness",

and Paul plainly considers it to be everyone's goal. Vatican Council II was of the same mind. All the faithful are to "taste fully of the paschal mysteries", and to burn with love during the Eucharistic Sacrifice (SC, 10). We are to "abound in contemplation" (LG, 41) and to be "thoroughly enriched with the treasures of mysticism" (AGD, 18).[1] Just as Scripture and patristic literature know nothing of the late arriving two-way theory, so also this last Council completely bypassed the theologians who held it. Rather we find clear mystical language applied to all classes of the faithful with no discrimination whatever.

Such likewise was the clear mind of Saint Teresa and Saint John. Each of these doctors of contemplation has fifteen or twenty powerful texts in which they make explicit their strong conviction that all of the faithful are called to the heights of infused prayer. Since this too will be discussed more adequately in another study, I shall here present a few samples only.[2] Saint John of the

[1] The last two citations refer immediately to priests and religious, but no theologian makes a distinction among states in life on the basis of the call to deep prayer. Hence, the texts may be applied to the married as well.

[2] This more complete volume will deal with two or three problematic texts which actually are concerned, not with normal cases, but with people who suffer impediments of one type or another. The well known chapter 17 of Saint Teresa's *Way of Perfection* is answered by the saint herself in chapter 19.

Cross lays it down as a basic principle, rooted in the very nature of God as pure love, that whatever he gives he gives completely: "the Father of lights [James 1:17] who is not closefisted but diffuses himself abundantly, as the sun does its rays without being a respecter of persons [Acts 10:34] wherever there is room."[3] No consistent theist can have a problem with this text, for it is a mere summation of the biblical revelation. In the context John is responding to people who consider descriptions of lofty prayer to be exaggerated, and he makes his point regarding the universal call to the heights in five ways: (a) God places no restrictions on his gifts; (b) whatever he gives he gives fully; (c) in the same manner as the sun shines indiscriminately on everything, so the Lord has no small favored elite; (d) there are no two ways, no two classes, for God loves everyone; (e) one condition only is required, namely, that each person is determined and prepared to provide the room for the gift to be given.

We may notice two texts in Saint John of the Cross that explicitly declare that the transforming union is meant for all men and women in every vocation:

---

[3] *The Living Flame of Love,* stanza 1, no. 15, translated by Kieran Kavanaugh and Otilio Rodriguez (Washington: Institute of Carmelite Studies, 1973), pp. 584–585.

If a man remains both faithful and retiring in the midst of these favors [the first bits of discursive meditation] the Lord will not cease raising him degree by degree until he reaches the divine union of transformation. . . . If the individual is victorious over the devil in the first degree, he will pass on to the second; and if so in the second, he will go on to the third and likewise through all the seven mansions.[4]

We should notice that Saint John has no doubts about the divine intention: ". . . the Lord *will not* cease raising him . . . he *will* pass on. . . ." When the saint writes of the most sublime prayer of the transforming union, the entering into the very spiration of the Holy Spirit, he cannot seem to contain himself: "O souls, created for these grandeurs and called to them! What are you doing? How are you spending your time?"[5] There is no ambiguity in Saint John's thought: he explicitly refers to all humans, baptized or not, and he declares them made for the transforming union and called to it. He could not be more straightforward and clear.

Yet at this point an obvious question arises: Why do so few people actually reach the heights of prayer to which they are called? Most of those

[4] *The Ascent of Mount Carmel,* book 2, chapter 11, no. 9; op. cit., p. 135.

[5] *The Spiritual Canticle,* stanza 39, no. 7; op. cit., p. 559.

who raise this question answer it in terms of the divine will. They attempt to get themselves out of an embarrassing corner by the remark, not really thought out, that God calls some to mystical contemplation and others he does not. Naturally enough, it is convenient that they place themselves in the latter category. Saint John of the Cross will have no part of this explanation. Explicitly raising the question, he declares:

> Here it should be pointed out why there are so few who reach this high state of union with God. It should be known that the reason is not because God wishes that there be only a few of these spirits so elevated; he would rather want all to be perfect, but he finds so few vessels that will endure so lofty and sublime a work . . . as a result he proceeds no further in purifying them.[6]

For the saint, the explanation lies entirely on the human level. God forces himself on no one. If we refuse to be purified and to live the gospel with complete generosity, we do not advance in prayer. Lest the reader think this may be a stray text, we may add one other in the same vein:

> When the soul frees itself of all things and attains to emptiness and dispossession concerning them, which is equivalent to what it can do of itself, it is impossible that God fail to do his part by com-

---

[6] *The Living Flame of Love*, stanza 2, no. 27; op. cit., p. 604.

municating himself to it at least silently and sec-
retly. It is more impossible than it would be for
the sun not to shine on clear and uncluttered
ground. As the sun rises in the morning and shines
upon your house so that its light may enter if
you open the shutters, so God, who is watching
over Israel, does not doze, nor still less sleep, will
enter the soul that is empty and fill it with divine
goods."[7]

Once again Saint John makes it clear that the explanation lies on the human level: *when* we free
ourselves . . . *if* we open the shutters . . . it is
impossible that God will not communicate himself fully. The saint's mind could not be more
lucid.

Even though Saint Teresa is just as emphatic
as is Saint John, we shall consider only three texts
out of perhaps a dozen and a half. In her *Interior
Castle,* the most mature of her works, she speaks
of laymen and women who in their married state
are living the gospel generously and without cut-
ting corners. They combine a serious prayer life
with devotion to duty and love of neighbor. Re-
marking that "there are many such souls in the
world", she observes that "there seems no reason
why they should be denied entrance to the very
last of the mansions; nor will the Lord deny them
this if they desire it, for their disposition is such

[7]Ibid., stanza 3, no. 46; pp. 627–628.

that he will grant them any favor."[8] The last of the mansions is, of course, the transforming union, and she sees no reason why fully generous laypeople should not reach it. In other words there is no restriction as to the call; there is no small elite. The only condition is the "if", that is, if they live with magnanimity. For Teresa, to desire a thing is to be fully determined to achieve it. In her vocabulary desire is no mere velleity. To one with proper dispositions God will give "any favor". Like John, Teresa cannot conceive a closefisted God who respects persons and gives in a limited manner.

When she comes to explain why so few actually reach the seventh mansion, the saint lays the total blame on the human level: "I cannot help feeling the pity of it when I see how much we are losing, and all through our own fault [she is speaking of the lofty prayer of the sixth mansion]. For, true though it is that these are things which the Lord gives to whom he will, he would give them to us all if we loved him as he loves us."[9] The reader will notice that her thought is identical with that of Saint John of the Cross: the final explanation of a failure to grow to the very heights is not

[8] *Interior Castle,* Mansion 3, chapter 1, translated by E. Allison Peers (New York: Doubleday, Image edition, 1961), p. 59.

[9] Ibid., Mansion 6, chapter 4; p. 154.

found in the divine will, for God fully gives to all who really want fullness. Her teaching includes that inevitable "if". Speaking of lofty prayer in her earlier autobiography, Teresa offers the same explanation. "Reflect that it is indeed certain that God gives himself in this way to those who give up all for him. He shows no partiality. He loves everyone. Nobody has any excuses."[10] The universal call to the summit of infused prayer could not be presented any more clearly, cogently, concisely. If there is mystery in all of this, it is how anyone could possibly think Teresa and John of the Cross thought otherwise.

Virginity is not only the fulfillment vocation par excellence. It is also the vocation of totality: entirety of self-gift in exchange for plenitude of return, the "much more". Because the virgin gives up earthly marriage and property for the kingdom, she sets out on a path of identification with Jesus that is as complete as is open to the human person. She is a virgin for the sake of the transforming union. Prayer is the primary purpose of her vows. Not just a little prayer, but the consummation of it.

Martha's sister, Mary, sitting at the Lord's feet undividedly drinking of him and his wisdom, is the perfect picture of virginity and contemplation.

[10]*Life*, chapter 27, no. 12, translated by Kieran Kavanaugh and Otilio Rodriguez (Washington: Institute of Carmelite Studies, 1976), p. 178.

While she does her due work at its appropriate time, she knows full well that the "one thing", the top priority in anyone's life, is gazing on the beauty of the Lord. And Jesus gives her his complete stamp of approval; her absorption in him is both the overriding necessity of life and the beginning in dark faith of what will be her eternal, enthralling destiny in clear vision—"it will not be taken from her" (Lk 10:38–42).

CHAPTER TWELVE

SIGNS OF THE VOCATION

Can a young man or woman know with a reason-
ably well-founded assurance that God is calling
him or her to consecrated chastity? Given that the
Lord does beckon "in a special way, through an
interior illumination" (an expression of Pope Paul
VI), we now ask just what this inner enlighten-
ment may be and what signs may accompany it.

Ordinarily the indications of a vocation to celibacy are neither flashy nor extraordinary. The interior illumination is not a vision, not a tap on
the shoulder, not a voice spoken in audible sound
waves. Not everyone is assailed, as was Saint Paul
on the road to Damascus, by a light and voice
from heaven (Acts 9:3–6). Yet we may still ask
whether there is some perception of the call, some
psychological awareness of the divine invitation.

The answer is yes, even though the awareness
may not be what the recipient might expect. We
may, therefore, profitably reflect on it. The young
person called to consecrated chastity will have a
greater than usual bent toward God, an attraction
to him. This young person will often readily see
that a mere earthly existence is insufficient, funda-

mentally unsatisfying, basically empty. He may indeed enjoy parties, dances, and dating, but they invariably leave him with a sense of incompleteness. Young women attract him but he senses that none of them, no matter how beautiful, will ever fill his heart. He wants more, much more.

We must return to what we spoke of earlier, virginity as fullness. The young person with this gift has been given by God, at least in an incipient degree, a love-gift, a focusing on God that excludes a similar centering on anyone else. This love-gift may be weak and dim at the beginning, but it is there.

This first sign will be accompanied by a second: an attraction to a particular celibate lifestyle (private dedication, secular institute, active or enclosed religious life), and/or a persuasion that God wants him in that form of dedication. Some youth feel a clear, strong attraction to the active or cloistered life and together with it, a strong persuasion that God wants them there. With these people there is little or no doubt about the matter. Others feel only the persuasion, more or less insistent, that God is inviting them. Their mind is that if he wants it, they are willing, even if a felt attraction is absent. The inner illumination of which Pope Paul speaks seems in this second group to be mostly an intellectual matter, whereas with the first group it is accompanied by a perceived drawing toward the life.

Sound motivation is the third sign of the virginal charism. Desiring celibacy for the reasons described here is a strong indication that one possesses this love-gift from God. The virgin does not have a negative view of sexuality, nor is she fleeing the sacrifices of marriage or the responsibilities of life in the world—these motives are inadequate. She is a woman in love and she is pursuing her Beloved with a greater freedom. She also wishes to do something to help her brothers and sisters reach God—either by a life of prayer, solitude, and penance or by a life of prayer and apostolic involvement.

The final sign is capability. When God gives the celibate gift, he also gives the physical, mental, and moral health necessary to actualize it in a specific lifestyle. Necessary health need not mean absolute perfection, but it does mean a basic sufficiency. Each institute determines the minimal capabilities required for its life and work.

Preparation in Prayer

The young woman and man called to celibacy are inclined by the beckoning Spirit to a more than minimal interest in prayer. If they are fully open to God's gifts, this inclination will be strong and persistent, and it will be actualized in practice. There is no better preparation for an eventual embracing of this vocation than a fervent, growing communion with him who is the whole purpose of the life. This private prayer will be fed and furthered by a vibrant liturgical life, by devotion to the first Virgin, by regular, well-chosen spiritual reading, and, when it is available, by competent spiritual direction.

CHAPTER THIRTEEN

WITNESS

It has always been true that most people are more effectively moved by actions than by words, but in an atmosphere in which we are bombarded by thousands of advertisements each day (so the statistics say) in both the electronic and printed media, words and claims fall largely on deaf ears—unless there are sincere deeds to back them up. Our sophisticated compatriots are simply unimpressed by the speech, even the polished proclamations, of mediocre men and women. When they see purity, fire, and selflessness, they take notice. They do not always follow, but they do notice.

Not for nothing does the new Code of Canon Law lay it down that the first apostolate of religious is not to operate schools, hospitals, and religious education programs. Their primary message is to be something, namely, to be saints, to remind the world of the matchless life of Christ, who alone is the healer the world so dreadfully needs. "The first apostolate of all religious is the testimony of their consecrated life, which [testimony] they are bound to foster by prayer and penance" (Canon 673).

Prayer and penance: not propaganda in the media, not demonstrations in the streets, not first of all "relevant works". First of all, prayer and penance: a lesson impossible to learn when one operates on secular principles, but easy to grasp when one is enlightened by the Spirit to see how human beings actually are sanctified and saved.

Why is gospel witness always first a *be* and then a *do*? (Mt 5:19; Acts 4:31; 6:4). One reason is that we are serving the God of truth, who demands authentic witnesses, people who are what they proclaim. Words unrooted in goodness are unworthy of him. Another reason is that without a serious prayer life we are likely to become cold, officious functionaries, who may do much work but little apostolate. Without depth in the speaker, words from the pulpit or in the classroom, at the bedside or on the street may be impeccably correct, but they leave the listener as hollow as the speaker. Then, too, the Christian must first of all be authentic because if he is not, the sham will eventually be found out, even if at the beginning a few did not detect it.

"Religious are to render to Christ and to the Church a *public* witness" (Canon 607, §3). Not all celibates are religious, and those who are not may or may not render public testimony. Members of secular institutes are often unknown as such in their daily round of professional duties, and women who live their consecrated virginity on a privately vowed basis are also for the most part unrecognized as consecrated. But religious are publicly ecclesial men and women who visibly represent the Church. Because they are to be readily identifiable, canon law requires that they wear a religious habit (Canon 669, §1, 2), and for the same reason priests are to wear clerical garb (Canon 284). Modern government and business understand the principle very well, and this is why they require their service personnel to wear a uniform dress as they go about their duties in hospitals, trains, buses, airplanes, restaurants, and banks as well as in the military and security branches of contemporary life. If identifying garb has its value in the secular sphere, it is even more needed in the sacred. The transcendent order of the divine is so widely neglected in our century that we desperately need living signs that God is indeed present among his people. One of the last things the world needs is to have consecrated people hide their identity, to dress and live like everyone else. When they do so conceal themselves in an anonymous lifestyle, their public witness is diluted and sometimes completely lost—another victory for the increased secularization of the human community in our twentieth century.

To what does the consecrated virgin witness? To answer this question we must assume the normal case: that one is living the vocation generously and fully. No mediocre person in any state of life is a testimony to the gospel's power and attractiveness. Supposing then that the virgin is what she ought to be, we find that her first witness is to the primacy of God in his creation. Almost no intelligent adult can miss the visible message that here is a woman so taken with God that he is the top priority in her life. She lays down her entire being in loving adoration of him. Worldlings may not like the message, and they may not follow her example, but the living statement is there. An eternal word has been powerfully spoken, and each observer will give an account of how he does or does not respond to it.

The celibate individual likewise gives testimony to genuine love of sisters and brothers. We have said earlier that virginity not only is compatible with warm human love, but that it increases it. A virgin full of prayer will radiate the love for others that we routinely find in the saints. The celibate Lord said that all men are to know his disciples when they see a love patterned after his own (Jn 13:34-35). People who may be little moved by philosophical and theological arguments are often affected by the sight of a Saint Francis kissing a leper or by hearing the parable of the father kissing and hugging the returned prodigal (Lk 15:20). The celibate man and woman are to image to the world this unspeakable love of the celibate Lord who has willed to call us brothers, sisters, and friends.

The faithful virgin also tells the world by her being and mode of life that none of us here has a lasting city, that we are not to be of this world, just as Jesus said that he was not of it (Jn 17:16). In her simple clothing, her disregard for jewelry and artificial makeup, her sparing or non-use of television and superficial amusements she proclaims unworldliness (1 Pet 3:3–5). Like Saint Paul she weeps at the behavior of the "enemies of the Cross of Christ" (Phil 3:18), and she declares by her life that no one has here a permanent abode, that we are pilgrims and should live like pilgrims (Heb 11:13–16).

She is also therefore a sign of the Cross and asceticism, of the hard road and the narrow gate that lead to life (Mt 7:13–14). Her life tells us that the kingdom does not consist in food and drink but in the joy, peace, and holiness given by the Spirit (Rom 14:17). This testimony is not, of course, popular. Indeed it is only too often in disfavor with the very celibates that should themselves be a sign of the Cross. This unpopularity is just what greeted the Master, for he himself said that few there are who choose to walk the hard road and enter the narrow gate. But the few are worth saving, and the celibate is a beacon for them.

The faithful virgin is a testimony to honesty in the midst of a faithless generation (Mt 12:39). In an age which takes deceit as a way of life and accepts as routine the violation of marriage commitments and even religious vows, the steadfast virgin is a model of fidelity to her word whether in the minor promises of daily life or the solemn pledges of a life commitment. Indeed, in an inspired portrayal of the final reckoning virginity stands for fidelity. The 144,000 virgins of Revelation 14:4 are the followers of Christ who have remained faithful to him. Virginity stands for fidelity, as adultery for idolatry.

The virgin is likewise a symbol of joy. All disciples in every vocation are called to "rejoice in the Lord always" (Phil 4:4), or as Saint Augustine brilliantly put it, to be an "alleluia from head to toe". Anyone full of love will be full of joy. The joy Jesus gives is not partial; it is full (Jn 15:11). Surely that woman or man who gives undivided attention to him, the very source of delight, can be nothing other than an incarnated alleluia. Sufferings there will be in any state of life, but the celibate Saint Paul is able to say that he overflows with joy in all of his many severe tribulations (2 Cor 7:4). One of the most attractive traits of the saints is their radiant peace and joy even in the bleakest and most forbidding of circumstances.

The virgin is a figure of final fulfillment. If she reminds the world that womanly attractiveness is not primarily bodily beauty, she also calls to mind that a woman is not a thing, a mere means to male pleasure. She proclaims in her being that woman has an independent personal dignity that transcends the fleeting allurements of a body destined to the disfigurement and dissolution of aging, illness, death. She proclaims that final bodily splendor will be the lot of the virtuous when they reign with Christ in the glory of their risen bodies.

The virgin therefore anticipates the final completion. She gives up in the bloom of youth what everyone gives up at the moment of death. The millionaire owns not a penny as he breathes his last. He is no longer married. He no longer disposes of himself in the wiggle of a finger. The virgin lives the paschal emptying from her youth and she derives a reward "many times over in this present age". She is the Church concentrated.

Because her whole life is undividedly centered on him who is the Way, the Truth, and the Life, this woman eminently witnesses to the faithful members of the Church who as "innocent and genuine, perfect children of God among a deceitful and underhanded brood shine in the world like bright stars, because they offer it the word of life" (Phil 2:15–16). The faithful virgin is indeed a star showing the way to all who want eternal enthrallment where alone it can be found.

CHAPTER FOURTEEN

CHARISM

The subtitle of this volume speaks of the virginal consecration as a charism, that is, a gift of the Holy Spirit given for the benefit of the whole ecclesial community. While this gift does benefit the individual recipient of it in all the ways we have traced out, it is of immense enrichment for the entire people who make up the Church. This endowment and adornment further the full development of all the faithful in that the virgin stands and lives in their midst as one who

— is more radically inserted into the paschal mystery, the death and resurrection of the Church's Lord;

— expresses visibly to the world the primacy of God in his creation, that he is worthy to be loved in and for himself and not merely as a kind of insurance policy in time of trouble;

— declares the person to *be* a praise of God and not simply one who works on his behalf;

— proclaims the primacy of contemplation, a deep immersion in the Trinity;

— provides a new visible witness to Christ himself praying, teaching, and healing;

— follows Christ more closely in his chastity, obedience, and poverty, a total belonging to the Father;
— declares that chastity is possible in all vocations;
— builds up the Mystical Body by her prayer, penance, and example;
— realizes therefore the mission of the Church and essentially belongs to her life and holiness;
— anticipates the eschatological fullness of life in the beatific vision and the risen body.

This complete self-gift to the divine Beloved, therefore, not only brings the hundredfold to the individual person, but it literally adorns the Church of God, herself richly described in Scripture as his virgin Bride. The celibate woman and man are persons whose whole attention is focused on Beauty, ever ancient, ever new, persons whose *raison d'être* is none other than a profound love covenant and communion with the Word and his Father through their Holy Spirit.

ABBREVIATIONS

AGD   *Ad gentes divinitus:* The Decree on the Church's Missionary Activity, Vatican II, December 7, 1965.

CD   *Christus Dominus:* The Decree on the Pastoral Office of Bishops in the Church, Vatican II, October 28, 1965.

LG   *Lumen gentium:* The Dogmatic Constitution on the Church, Vatican II, November 21, 1964.

OT   *Optatam totius:* The Decree on the Training of Priests, Vatican II, October 28, 1965.

PC   *Perfectae caritatis:* The Decree on the Up-to-date Renewal of Religious Life, Vatican II, October 28, 1965.

PO   *Presbyterorum ordinis:* The Decree on the Life and Ministry of Priests, Vatican II, December 7, 1965.

SC   *Sacrosanctum concilium:* The Constitution on the Sacred Liturgy, Vatican II, December 4, 1963.